Y0-CAS-140

HIGH ROCK
AND THE
GREENBELT

This rock and the loosestrife swamp nearby were among John Mitchell's and Gretta Moulton's favorite places. For many decades, park stewards and visionaries have come across this mighty boulder as they set out to explore High Rock and the Staten Island Greenbelt. They provided a sacred place for contemplation, keeping watch over the Greenbelt and awaiting the next generation of visitors.

HIGH ROCK AND THE GREENBELT

The Making of New York City's Largest Park

by John G. Mitchell

edited by
Charles E. Little

illustrated by
Marbury Brown

with photographs by
Dorothy Reilly

Center Books on American Places
George F. Thompson, series founder
and director

The Center for American Places
at Columbia College Chicago

All royalties from the sale of this book support the program of the Greenbelt Conservancy in Staten Island (www.sigreenbelt.org).

See the *Editor's Preface* (pages xi–xiii) for how this book came to be.

Original text (*Part One*) copyright © 1976 by John G. Mitchell, reproduced by permission of Alison C. Mitchell, executor, the estate of John G. Mitchell.

Original drawings (*Part One*) copyright © 1976 by Marbury Brown, reproduced by permission of Dorothy Brown, executor, the estate of Marbury Brown.

New material (*Part Two*) copyright © 2011 The Center for American Places at

Columbia College Chicago.

New photographs by Dorothy Reilly (front matter and *A Greenbelt Gallery*) copyright © 2011 Dorothy Reilly.

All rights reserved. No text, map, or photograph may be used or reproduced in any form or medium without written permission.
Published in 2011. First Edition.
Printed in China on acid-free paper.

The Center for American Places at Columbia College Chicago
600 South Michigan Avenue
Chicago, Illinois 60605-1996, U.S.A.
www.americanplaces.org

19 18 17 16 15 14 13 12 11   1 2 3 4 5

Library of Congress Cataloging-in-Publication Data
Mitchell, John G.
High Rock and The Greenbelt : the making of New York City's largest park / by John G. Mitchell / edited by Charles E. Little ; illustrated by Marbury Brown with photographs by Dorothy Reilly.—1st ed.
    p. cm.
 Includes bibliographical references and index.
 Rev. ed. of: High Rock. Originally published: New York : Friends of High Rock, 1976.
 ISBN 978-1-935195-20-7 (alk. paper)
 1. High Rock Park (New York, N.Y.)––History. 2. Greenbelt, The (New York, N.Y.)—History. 3. Staten Island (New York, N.Y.)—History. I. Little, Charles E. II. Brown, Marbury Hill, 1925- III. Mitchell, John G. High Rock. IV. Title.
 F127.S7M68 2011   –
 974.7'26--dc22
                        2010033066

for Gretta Moulton
1911–1971

Recreational development
is a job not of building
roads into lovely country,
but of building receptivity
into the still
unlovely human mind.

—Aldo Leopold

The Greenbelt is known for many things—from environmental education to carousel rides—but the abundance of natural areas along with tracts of undisturbed land designated "Forever Wild" by the New York City Department of Parks and Recreation define this special place. By Walker Pond in High Rock Park visitors may observe dragonflies, egrets, turtles, and a host of migrating birds in this truly wild spot.

CONTENTS

There is a certain sense of freedom children experience when they explore the Greenbelt. The woodlands and wetlands are low-tech and high-beauty. Imaginations are in full throttle when youngsters contemplate a horizon line without structures obscuring the view; when the distant sound of a woodpecker or owl fills the forest; and when trees grow taller than buildings. The Greenbelt remains the way nature intended. It is an ancient place to which young people are drawn. "Childhood decides," wrote Jean-Paul Sartre.

AUTHOR'S ACKNOWLEDGMENTS

In a sense, the making of this book has been a work of collaboration, and I am in heavy hock to the collaborators who added their invaluable pieces to the mosaic that we have here. I thank them all, with only two regrets. First, that I cannot name everyone who did help; second, that traditional acknowledgments are so inadequate a measure of the time and effort and care contributed by so many generous people.

I am especially indebted to the members of the High Rock staff—to Ethel Dicke, Olivia Hansen, Mildred Becker, Rudolph Lindenfeld, Elliot Willensky, and Mae Seeley—for their enduring patience and cooperation at times not always best suited to their own schedules.

Likewise, the staff and trustees of the Staten Island Institute of Arts and Sciences; in particular George O. Pratt, Jr., and Elsie Verkuil, for sharing recollections of High Rock's earliest days as a conservation center; Bradford Greene and Richard Buegler, for enlightening instruction in the physiography of the place; and Gail Schneider, for serving as my trusted pathfinder through an archival labyrinth of eighteenth- and nineteenth- century lore.

For perspectives from beyond High Rock's immediate institutional family, my thanks to Margaret Wood, Eleanor Bernheim, June Farmer, Livingston Francis, Albert V. Maniscalco, Alison Mitchell, and Horace Moulton.

A very special mention must be made of the original research contributed by Jean Halloran and Paul Cooper, whose earlier peregrinations through the history of the High Rock site provided a solid foundation for this work. Their work in tracing the pattern of land ownership over the years was aided by Wesley W. Braisted. In turn, Mr. Braisted was assisted by Albert L. Risi, of the Title Guarantee Company.

There are "Friends" to thank also: Gloria Benbow, Roberta Braisted, Gunda Halloran, Frances Hellinghausen, Fay Radin, and

Wesley Truesdell—the Friends of High Rock who persevered through difficult times to assure the publication of this book.

And, finally, a special salute to Cynthia Jacobson, who first conceived the idea for such a book; and to Elizabeth Seder, who, as editor, skillfully guided (and occasionally, perforce, guarded) the project from uncertain beginnings to the fulfilling end.

JOHN G. MITCHELL
Staten Island, New York
August 1976

A word to the wise: The opinions expressed in this work, not to mention occasional exhortations, are solely those of the author and in no way are intended to reflect the policies or positions, private or public, of the High Rock staff, The Friends of High Rock, or the Staten Island Institute of Arts and Sciences.

EDITOR'S PREFACE

In 1976, the influential journalist, writer, and editor John G. Mitchell published a little book on behalf of saving a precious part of Staten Island, New York, where he, his wife, Alison, and their two children had lived for many years. The book, *High Rock: A Natural and Unnatural History,* delightfully illustrated by the celebrated artist Marbury Brown, also a Staten Islander, was printed and distributed by The Friends of High Rock to great acclaim.

As it turned out, High Rock had many friends, and its preservation led, after intense civic activity, to the creation of the Staten Island Greenbelt (hereafter referred to as the Greenbelt), New York City's largest park and one of North America's largest big-city parks. And to many, Mitchell's book about saving High Rock has become an environmental classic, for it tells the story of one of the significant land conservation achievements in the United States, ranking with the battles for Storm King Mountain along the Hudson River, which ultimately led to the passage of the Environmental Policy Act of 1969; or Echo Park in Colorado, where citizens stopped profligate dam-building; or the many other treasured American landscapes in a line that goes back to the struggle by John Muir during the nineteenth century to save the Sierra Nevada wilderness.

As a way to celebrate the High Rock story, and as a fitting tribute to John Mitchell, who died in 2007, and to those who worked with him on High Rock and the Greenbelt and who are no longer with us, Alison Mitchell, Mitch's wife of fifty-three years, and daughters Katherine and Pamela, asked me, as a long-time colleague and family friend, to bring High Rock up to date and see to its republication thirty-five years later by George F. Thompson and the Center for American Places at Columbia College Chicago. This book, *High Rock and the Greenbelt: The Making of New York City's Largest Park*, is the result.

What has become Part One of this new edition constitutes a reprinting of the original volume, with the wonderful drawings by Marbury Brown intact. John Mitchell's friend (and mine), the late Robert Hagenhofer, designed *High Rock*, and we have remained as faithful as we can to his original conception.

Part Two brings the story up to date through the collaborative effort of various organizations and many dedicated people. In this section is my overview essay (*Staten Island Green*) of the status of the Greenbelt today, which is followed by a portfolio of recent photographs (*A Greenbelt Gallery*) by Dorothy Reilly and then an edited proceedings (*A Greenbelt Forum*), organized and moderated by Deborah Popper. The book concludes with *A Greenbelt Directory*, by Michael Twomey (with research assistance by Joseph Ferlazzo of the New York City Department of Parks and Recreation), which describes the constituent properties and features of the Greenbelt, followed by biographical notes on those who created the original High Rock and those who have worked on this expanded version.

None of this would have been possible without the help of the staff of the Greenbelt Conservancy, notably former Executive Director Adena Long, staff members Dorothy Reilly and Tony Rho, Kathleen Vorwick, current President of the Board of Directors, and former board president Sally Williams and board member Michael Dominowski. The New York City Department of Parks and Recreation (www.nycgovparks.org) has also had a major hand in the creation of this book, notably via Thomas Paulo, the department's commissioner for Staten Island, who has led the modern effort to bring a fully realized greenbelt into being as well as to create a world-class system of parks and open spaces throughout Staten Island. The College of Staten Island (CSI), a unit of the City University of New York, provided major support to the project, especially in the persons of Deborah Popper, the nationally recognized geographer who is responsible for A Greenbelt Forum; Richard Flanagan, Professor of Political Science and Director of the CSI's Staten Island Project, which provided a generous grant for the forum; CSI Archivist James Kaser, who is setting up a special section on the Greenbelt; and Tomás Morales, President of the College.

Of special note in this cast of helpful characters is, of course, Alison Mitchell, who initiated the republication project and who provided guidance throughout. And much recognition is also owed to

Bradford Greene, who, more than anyone else, is surely the "father of the Greenbelt" for it was he who organized the Staten Island Citizens Planning Committee during the early 1960s that got everything started. His inspiring leadership has ramified in remarkable ways across a half-century of open space activism on Staten Island.

CHARLES E. LITTLE
Placitas, New Mexico
1 March 2011

PART ONE
HIGH ROCK: A NATURAL AND UNNATURAL HISTORY (1976)

FOREWORD

The story in this book is about a place, a program, an idea, and the evolution of all three. The place is High Rock Park Conservation Center, a seventy-two-acre woodland in the heart—at the buckle, if you will—of the Staten Island Greenbelt. The program is educational. It is concerned with the total environment—both the part that is natural and the part that has been molded and shaped by people. The idea is that, no matter how well we may mold and shape our human environment, we still need the other kind; and that, by having it or at least some remnant wild shreds of it, we inevitably will be better people.

If you have not yet been to High Rock, stop here. Put the book down. Put on a pair of old shoes. And go. Unlike so many other places, you will not be able to see High Rock through the windshield of your car. You will have to get out of your car and walk. Nothing strenuous, mind you. Just a quiet stroll in the woods. Just you and your senses. Then return to the book. Then, I hope, you will find more meaning in it.

Trail bridge at the loosestrife swamp.

A FINE PATCH OF WILD

It was October when I saw it first. Oak leaves turning brown in the warmth of Indian summer, maples edged with scarlet on the flats of the loosestrife swamp. Long shadows across a blacktop road winding up through deep woods. Sunbather's sky. The sound of wind in the treetops. The cry of a blue jay, the caw of a crow. The smell of drying humus, like straw, after rain. The photographer with me was clearly impressed. He stood in a shaft of sunlight at the edge of the road, in city cloth and Sunday shoes, and after a while he said something that others since have expressed in one manner of speaking or another, that future first-timers will undoubtedly sense as long as the place prevails. "For New York City," the photographer said, "it's a fine patch of wild." And it sure enough was that. By some miracle of human vision and natural tenacity, it still is.

For the six years preceding that discovery, I had lived on Staten Island, had poked into a few of its lingering woods here and there but had never once guessed that such a place as this could still be found. Not just in New York City. On Staten Island. The [Verrazano] Narrows Bridge had just been opened to Brooklyn. Wherever we remembered open lands before, we saw houses rising from the raw, red, clean-shaven earth; and we expected the same for the places we had never seen. On Hagstrom's official borough map, the hilly country north from Egbertville was stitched with streets. I had no idea then how maps can lie. Later, and somewhat wiser, I would understand more about phantom subdivisions and nonexistent roads. But, at the time, I saw only the stitches and did not go there, thinking the land was already sewn up in concrete. And on the ferryboats from Manhattan on Friday nights, we watched the scouts—boys and girls—toting packs and bedrolls to Staten Island. It never occurred to me to inquire where exactly it was they intended to camp when they got to the other side.

The girls, of course, were heading for High Rock, up the winding blacktop to that patch of wild spread in the shape of a butterfly across the southeast shoulder of Todt Hill. They had been doing this almost every weekend for more than ten years. Thousands of them, city girls mainly from Brooklyn and lower Manhattan, had made the crossing to camp among the oaks and maples. But now all of this was to end, for the camp's proprietors had decided to sell High Rock to a developer and bus their charges to other camps upstate. The scout leaders of Staten Island were understandably perturbed, as were a number of other individuals who valued High Rock as open space and who much preferred butterflies to ragged seams on the shoulders of Todt Hill. The photographer and I had been dispatched across the bay to chronicle the rumpus for the *New York Journal-American*.

We were greeted that afternoon by several women who had been active as volunteers in the program at High Rock and were now devoting their considerable efforts to keeping the camp open and the land intact. The strain of their ongoing struggle with the Girl Scout Council's executive committee was beginning to show. One woman appeared on the verge of tears as she told us how much High Rock had come to mean in the lives of girl scouts from the Lower East Side. "I know land is valuable on Staten Island," she said. "I know people need places to live. But, golly," and now she was swallowing hard, "you also need places to grow."

Then the woman with the blue eyes spoke. I do not recall her exact words, but I do remember thinking that she was surely someone to be reckoned with when the chips were down, as they were now. I put her name in my notebook, and her phone number, and at the end of the day I said I would call her from time to time over the next few weeks to stay in touch with new developments. As things turned out, I stayed in touch with Gretta Moulton—and with all the good events that were to happen as a result of her leadership—for the next seven years.

Hers was no solo effort, not by a long shot. There were others who helped. But it was she who involved them, nudged, cajoled, inspired, and impressed them, directed their talents to the jobs that needed to be done. Until her death in 1971, Gretta Moulton devoted a good part of her life to High Rock—rallied the civic troops to snatch the land from the developers, guided its transition to an environmental education center of national landmark status, fought long and hard to en-

Loosestrife.

Glacial erractic at the loosestrife swmp.

sure its adequate funding, held the meddlers and bunglers at bay. "She was our Joan of Arc," someone remarked to me after her death. The woman with the blue eyes would have blushed to hear that or laughed. Yet the more I think about that adulation, the closer it seems to come to the mark.

There is a part of High Rock that Gretta Moulton fancied more than any other—the loosestrife swamp, in the northern wing of the butterfly. A salubrious spot in all seasons, no doubt the favorite of others, including myself. A trail loops away from the blacktop, not far from High Rock's Nevada Avenue entrance, and soon you are into the woods on the edge of the swamp: red maples and highbush blueberries, pepperbush and chokeberry, skunk cabbage and Canada mayflower, azaleas and arrowhead, and (in the swamp) the purple loosestrife itself. And at the far end of the swamp, a large boulder—a glacial erratic, as the geologists say—carried here by the ice thousands of years ago. You touch the rock and you wonder, from where? The rock does not answer. The rock does not care. Still, the rock is a good place to sit and wonder about many things. About the ice; and the large shaggy animals that roamed here before and possibly after the ice; and how the forest slowly changed as the days of the millennia grew longer and warmer; and when it might have been that the first Indian, following a brook upstream from the salt marsh at the island's edge, came upon this same rock, wondering himself, then kneeling to drink from the pond that would not be a swamp for another 2,000 years. And about the men in red jackets who arrived by sea only 200 years ago, and the one or two or more who may have sat here also, watching their compatriots topple the tall trees for firewood and fortifications. And about the man known as "Professor Bugs," who covered so much of the island afoot that he must have sat here himself—this being fifty or seventy-five years ago—and thought to himself what a fine patch of wild this almost-swamp most certainly was.

Sitting on the rock at the far end of the loosestrife swamp, I find it easier to think about the past than the future. The future is such a far piece off. Of the future, you can be certain of only a very few things. The rock, for instance. It will be smaller tomorrow than it is today. You won't be able to measure that, but it's true. And the swamp, after many tomorrows, will be gone altogether, filled in with the bulk of its own natural decay. As for this butterfly of open space, this High Rock—who can say? It could be gone, too, stitched up in ragged seams. But only if we, in our individual lifetimes, allow it to happen. I do not think that we will.

Butterfly, sketched afield.

FIRE AND ICE

Once upon a time—say, about half a billion years ago—it was quite a different kind of place. Life was young and invertebrate then and wet. In the shallow Paleozoic sea, tiny organisms flourished and died and drifted down one upon the other, and the dusts and sands of the earth itself were fused with them, layer after layer on the ocean floor. Then the seabed slowly emerged through receding waters, and the exposed sediments baked in the oven of the sun and were rock. Schist, we would call it in our own time—the basement of the house of life as we know it at High Rock today.

The house was a long time abuilding. Two, three hundred million years slip by, and now there are dinosaurs at the front door, and the sky is gray with volcanic ash. The earth-house trembles from the fire within it. The rocks crack vertically. Along what is now the eastern half of Staten Island, the rocks are uplifted; to the west, they slump. Now there is a high jagged escarpment with some diabase and sandstone protruding but mostly black-gray serpentine laced with magnetite, the oxide of iron.

Periods and epochs, up through the Cretaceous, the Eocene, the Miocene, the Pliocene, the Pleistocene. And then the ice. Two great sheets grinding down from the north, covering all the first time; the second, the one called Wisconsin, terminating with its moraine heaped high along the eroded escarpment. The final architectural touch. Only yesterday, 20,000 years ago. The ice retreats. The land is littered with boulders. The new forest springing from the peat is boreal, all spruce and fir. In the hollows, ice pillars fractured from the receding glacier melt in the sun to form a chain of ponds, or kettles, along the top of the escarpment. The days grow warmer. The conifers grow sparser, succeeded by birch. In time, the birch succeeds to oak and hickory; the oak and hickory to hemlock and maple and beech, to the forest primeval, the climax community which can be altered now only by fire or new ice. Or the axe.

Having been axed a number of times over the past 200 years, the High Rock forest today is neither climactic nor primeval, though it probably contains some of the oldest trees remaining anywhere in New York City. The predominant species are oak: red, black, white, scarlet, pin, swamp, and chestnut. Next in number is the sweet gum, with its star-shaped leaves and spiky brown seed pods. Of hickories there are several varieties, mostly pignut and mockernut, but also a few shagbarks and bitternuts. Maple and beech run a close third; and, with some hemlock prevailing on the north and west slopes, the process of succession to a climax forest appears to be at work again. We shall never see such a forest in our time. But, with luck and no interference by human bunglers, our twenty-ninth-century descendents may. In the meantime, the sub-climax condition will continue to provide much diversity of tree types, with gray and black birch, tupelo (sour gum), ash, black walnut, and wild cherry, not to mention the tulip tree, of which some specimens on the lower south-facing slopes are taller and of greater girth than the venerable centenarian giants—what few that are left—of any other species.

In addition, a few exotics are to be found at High Rock, the legacy of seed-dropping birds and of runaway landscaping from Moravian Cemetery nearby. The aliens include the Japanese cork tree, the Chinese ailanthus (or Tree-of-Heaven), the Austrian pine, and the ginkgo.

Because of the shade of the forest canopy and the acidic nature of the oak-mulch soils, the understory is not altogether lush. But it is certainly diverse: ironwood, dogwood, spicebush, blackberry, wild grape, Virginia creeper, royal and cinnamon ferns, trout lily, and poison ivy, among other woody and herbaceous species.

The succession of fauna is less easily cataloged. Evidence of the presence of Pleistocene shaggies hereabouts is scant, though Staten Island historians Charles W. Leng and William T. Davis (alias Professor Bugs, so-called because of his scientific fascination with insects) reported that mastodon teeth were uncovered in nearby Moravian Cemetery, at a depth of twenty-three feet, in 1899. With the passing of the larger mammals, one guesses the land soon enough was inherited by modern creatures, such as deer and black bear and bobcat and beaver and, going back a ways, possibly wolves and woodland buffalo,

William T. Davis, from photographs.

for all we know. It would be nice to think so. But, unlike the mastodon, which likely succumbed more to climatic change than to stone-age weapons, the latter animals went under shortly after Europeans arrived in the New World and proceeded to tame it with their axes and firesticks.

A number of smaller mammals managed to survive the taming (or, in some cases, learned to thrive from it). Raccoon on occasion skulk through the High Rock woods, though one is rarely seen. The marsupial opossum is more common, as is the muskrat when water conditions are favorable to its building of nests in the ponds. There are chipmunks and shrews and field mice and a proliferating population of gray squirrels and cottontail rabbits. Of cold-blooded creatures there are salamanders, turtles, and such small harmless serpents as the garter and water snake.

Not all of the birds encountered at High Rock are permanent residents. The raptors, of course, are year-rounders—the screech owl, sparrow hawk, and red-tailed hawk. So are the pheasant and quail, the downy and hairy woodpecker, the crow and blue jay, the nuthatch and chickadee, the starling and sparrow, the finch and the cardinal. In the spring, the avian ranks are swelled by such migrants as the wood duck,

Raccoon

mourning dove, ruby-throated hummingbird, robin, wood thrush, cedar waxwing, grackle, red-winged blackbird, Baltimore oriole and yellow warbler, green and great blue heron. In the winter come the junco and the evening grosbeak, among others. Altogether, more than sixty bird species have been observed at High Rock over the years.

"Air, water, soil, and fire," writes microbiologist René Dubos, "the rhythms of nature and the variety of living things, are not of interest only as chemical mixtures, physical forces, or biological phenomena; they are the very influences that have shaped human life." So they are. But often the process can work in the other direction, too—human life influencing the rhythms and varieties of nature, as it has at High Rock, for better or for worse, since humankind first planted its heavy foot there.

Opossum

British landing, Staten Island, July 1776.

TRACKS

U nless Schoolcraft and other early scholars were mistaken, the local Indians, the Leni-Lenape, did not care much for Staten Island. The Lenape called it *Aquehonga Monockong*, the place of the bad woods and, except for occasional hunting forays inland, preferred to stay near the shore, taking their protein from shellfish. What it was about the woods that bothered the Indians is anyone's guess. Bad spirits, possibly, or dark mythic tales from the edge of the council fire, or perhaps plain poor hunter's luck; though the Great Spirit only knows how the Lenape tried, putting the torch to the forest here and there to drive the game toward the waiting bowmen, or sometimes just burning a hole in the woods—primitive wildlife managers that they were—to improve the forage for deer. Or perhaps they became disenchanted when they saw what the early Dutch settlers were up to. The Dutch, not to mention the Huguenots and the Waldensians, who were skillful at burning charcoal, were making monockong with axes in the tall timber.

To what extent the Dutch addressed their axes to the forest of Todt Hill is beyond historical recall. It may have been that they were more interested at the time in its ore deposits, for history does recall that the Dutch referred to this promontory as Yserbert, or Iron Hill. Later, or perhaps simultaneously, the prevailing word *Todt* became associated with the hill as the result of an unfriendly encounter there between Dutch and Indians, a dispute over mining and forestry practices, possibly. Whatever the provocation, an unspecified number of Dutchmen perished in the argument, so that Todt, or Death Hill, came into popular usage.[1]

The Dutch were not outstandingly successful on their Staaten Eylant. One Michael Pauw was granted a Dutch West India Company charter to the entire island in 1630, but he soon surrendered his rights without exercising them. Then came David DeVries, whose small plantation fell to ruin in the Pig War of 1641, so called because of yet another bloody dispute with the Indians, this time over the lawful ownership of hogs. By the 1660s, the Dutch were more than happy to pass the island into English hands. And Governor Francis Lovelace, in 1670, sought to settle the Indian disputes once and for all. To an elaborate barbecue in Manhattan, he summoned the chiefs of the Lenape. Lovelace told them he was buying the place of the bad woods. The Lenape said that was fine with them, but that the price of the land had gone up since they had relinquished Manhattan to the Dutch for twenty-four dollars and a song. There undoubtedly was much dickering back and forth, but eventually the shrewd Briton closed the deal with a gift of 400 fathoms of wampum, sixty barrels of lead, thirty axes, twenty guns, and a firkin of powder, among sundry other concessions. For their part, the Indians retained the right to harvest ash and hickory on the island for their baskets and canoes. Lovelace may have been pleased with himself, but from the long perspective of history it was a bad deal for posterity. Land values on the island have been spiraling upward ever since.

High Rock, if one may so prematurely apply that twentieth-century name, was not much affected by human activity in the early colonial period. It is recorded, nevertheless, that the land was formally mapped and patented shortly after Lovelace's acquisition of the island and that, by 1687, under the system of British Crown Grants then in vogue, at least four individuals held title to tracts in the High Rock area. Lewis Lakeman and Francis Martinow each owned about a hundred acres. William Stillwell, who for a time resided in the Stillwell-Perrine house (now an official landmark) on Reed's Brook at Richmond Road in New Dorp, held a grant of sixty acres. And John Palmer was lord of a vast manor, some 5,100 acres stretching across the island to Kill Van Kull. In the spring of that year, Palmer conveyed his manor to Thomas Dongan, "Governor of the Province of New York and Territories depending thereon in America and his most Sacred Majesty, James the Second, by the Grace of God, of England." And Dongan promptly named it the Lordshippe of Cassiltowne.

Over the years, Dongan's land and other adjacent manors were subdivided into smaller parcels, and on the deeds appeared the names of some of the island's most illustrious early families: Butler and Parker and Micheau and Jerris and Clawson and Vanderbilt and Burger and Everingham. And Conner, the Irishman who arrived in 1760 with enough hard cash to purchase more than 300 acres in the Lordshippe of Cassiltowne. Heavily forested, the parcel ran north from the Mills Dale (Buck's Hollow) up the south shoulder of Todt Hill. Conner soon prospered, dammed the stream draining the dale and the Black Horse Ravine (as well as the loosestrife swamp and Walker Pond at High Rock), and built beside the resulting pool a small but sturdy sawmill. The millpond was located a short distance downhill from what is now the intersection of Rockland Avenue and Manor Road; Connor's homestead was northwest of it (now the woods of Seaview Hospital). Rockland was then known as Conner's Road. The stream, which we call Richmond Brook, was named in Conner's day for the sawmill.

Richard Conner went about his business in a quiet and efficient way, logging his land selectively for whatever timbers and boards his neighbors might have required, which could not have been much in the way of wood since there were so few in the way of neighbors. Conner was an efficient politician as well, for in 1766 he was elected to the Board of County Supervisors, and later he was among the island's representatives to the First Continental Congress. He missed the second congress, assembled in Philadelphia in the early summer of 1776, and presumably was about his island business on the second and third days of July even as Benjamin Franklin and John Adams were editing Thomas Jefferson's final draft of the Declaration of Independence, the two of them puzzling, perhaps, over the Virginian's theory of natural rights:

> *When in the course of human events, it becomes necessary for one people to . . . assume among the powers of the earth, the separate and equal station to which the laws of nature and of nature's God entitle them . . . .*

And, on those same two days of 1776, the people of Staten Island, Conner among them, could look out from their shores upon the fluttering flags of the British fleet and on whaleboats filled with the red tunics of Sir William Howe's light infantry and grenadiers. Within forty-eight hours, 9,000 British troops had come ashore, outnumbering the colonial residents three-to-one. Within a week, the nine were joined by 20,000 more. On Staten Island, the laws of nature would have to wait.

As a staging area for British expeditions against the Continental forces on Long Island and in New Jersey, Staten Island occupied a strategic niche through the early years of the Revolutionary War. And at the heart of the niche, or very close to it, was High Rock. Two miles to the southwest were the heavily fortified Richmond Redoubts at Ketchum's Hill. Lookouts were stationed at Lighthouse Hill and Dongan's Knoll (Ocean Terrace and Todt Hill Road) and possibly in the tall trees on the Todt Hill ridge overlooking Raritan Bay, directly above the iron mines from which the British were busy extracting ore for ship anchors and cannonballs.[2] And almost within spitting distance of The Rock, more than a few clandestine rebels and some reluctant Tories being so inclined, was the headquarters of Sir William Howe himself, at the Rose and Crown Tavern (New Dorp Land and Richmond Road).

Also nearby (at Amboy and Richmond roads) was the Black Horse Tavern, then operated by the great-grandmother of Cornelius Vanderbilt. British officers from Howe's general staff were billeted at the Black Horse, and it is said the taproom there was frequented by American spies eager to take advantage of every rum-loosened slip of an English lip. Thus informed, the rebel agents would ride away into the night, up the Egbertville Ravine along Conner's Sawmill Brook, High Rock to the right of them, Buck's Hollow to the left, and then turn to the north into Black Horse Ravine (also called Bloodroot Valley), and on past Jones's Wolf Pit to the Committee of Safety meeting at the Christopher House, or even farther, across the great swamp and the Arthur Kill to the surer safety of General Washington's New Jersey outposts.

The hills around High Rock were white in those early war years—first white with the snows of winter, then white with the summer sailcloth tents of the British troops, bivouacked in the blazing sun, their natural shade, the forest canopy, whacked up for fuel and reduced to ashes. For such landowners as Richard Conner there would be no more selective logging until the British were gone and by some accounts not even then, since there would be so little timber to choose from. On behalf of their own troops, Christopher Billopp's loyalist militia, and the British commands in lower Manhattan, Howe and his generals had ordered the island's landowners and magistrates to "cut and cart to the most contiguous landing such proportion of their woods as will fully answer the intent and meaning of this proclama-

Black Horse Tavern.

Christopher House.

tion, and prevent the disagreeable necessity of granting permissions for their woods to be cut by others."

Such a permission was apparently granted to Conner, whose Todt Hill lands were already at the disposal of the British and, more than likely, shorn of much of their timber early on in the occupation. With British blessings, therefore, Conner proceeded to "cut and cart" woods belonging to Samuel and John Broome, two prominent patriots who had fled to Connecticut after Howe's arrival. As measure of the magnitude of the British demands on the forests of central Staten Island, it is recorded that Conner removed from the Broome woods, near Fresh Kills, some 6,000 cords of oak, beech, birch, maple, cedar, and chestnut.[3] And though the Revolutionary archives fail to render further evidence of Conner's forced participation in the clear-cutting of the island, it is more than likely that his sawmill was much in demand in the fall of 1778 after Lt. Colonel John Simcoe arrived at the Richmond Redoubts to relieve a "sickly" regiment, found the veterans living in huts "wretchedly made of mud," ordered these "thrown down" and put his Queen's Rangers to work building "ranges of log houses."

The departure of the British soldiers and the end of the war brought only a temporary respite to the shriveled woods, for logging of one kind or another was resumed in the early 1800s and continued intermittently through the century. In 1887, geologist Arthur Hollick, colleague of Leng and Davis, would be compelled to note ruefully in the proceedings of the Natural Science Association that there was "hardly a patch of woodland left on the island of more than fifty years' growth." O, there were a few lusty survivors here and there, Hollick reported. A chestnut with a circumference of eighteen feet, a sour gum ten feet around, and a white oak he estimated to be 230 years of age. But none of these were in the woodlands of Todt Hill. It was *Aquehonga Monocknong* all over again, and, inasmuch as ship-building was a thriving industry on Staten Island, and ship builders then preferred oak, monocknong would continue to prevail right into the twentieth century. As late as 1924, Leng and Davis observed in their history of the island and its people, there was "a sawmill in Buck's Hollow with a temporary village for its employees."

Of notable events that may have occurred in or near the recovering High Rock woodlands in the middle and late years of the nineteenth century, the record holds scant evidence. These were quiet

Sawmill in Buck's Hollow (Mills Dale), from a photograph, circa 1916.

years—a little logging here, some marginal hardscrabble farming there. Much of the land was left to its own natural processes, and the tracks one now discerns through the web of time are those of people who went to the forest, walking softly, to see if they could not learn what it had to teach.

It is unabashed speculation to suppose that Henry David Thoreau himself may once have made tracks across the High Rock perimeter. The proper historian, bridling at conjecture, would be inclined to say: "How do you know that he did that?" To which I, borrowing a bit from Thoreau's own brand of feisty logic, would have to respond: "How do you know that he didn't?" What we do know in any event is that Thoreau came to Staten Island in 1843 and stayed a year as tutor to the nephews of his Concord crony, Ralph Waldo Emerson. And from the Snuggery, a low brown farmhouse at the foot of the hill now bearing the Emerson name, Thoreau sallied forth from time to time to explore the island's wilder parts, notably the great marsh at Fresh Kills, where he spent at least one pleasant day on Lake's Island, collecting arrowheads.

Now, certainly, any sensible rambler setting forth from The Clove would have followed the Richmond Plank Road, past Howe's old head-quarters to Richmondtown, at the head of Fresh Kills. But was Thoreau a sensible rambler? I doubt it. I rather suspect Thoreau stayed away from the road, kept to the high ground from Emerson Hill south, then along the escarpment of Todt Hill, past the glacial ponds and through the woods on the hill's south shoulder, across Richmond Brook to Lighthouse Hill, to Ketchum's Hill, and down into the marsh. Thoreau would have been—the entire way—in the kind of rough tumbling country he preferred. Give or take a few hundred yards, such a course would surely have carried his tracks across High Rock.

The attractions of the "Middletown Forest," as the Todt Hill woodlands were soon to be called, did not escape the attention of another nineteenth-century visitor, Frederick Law Olmsted, the landscape architect and designer of great urban parks. Actually, he was more than a visitor. For several years before his appointment as architect-in-chief of Central Park, Olmsted farmed a 130-acre tract in the Woods of Arden, on Raritan Bay. The farm was a failure, no doubt in part because its owner spent much of his time writing letters to distant friends, extolling the glories of Staten Island. "I do exceedingly enjoy the view," he allowed in one epistle, adding, "sometimes it is wondrous beautiful." In 1871, Olmsted served as consultant to the Staten Island Improvement Commission. Among the various areas within the scope of his studies was the Middletown Forest, with its chain of ponds like pearls on a necklace. In the commission's report that year, Olmsted proposed that the forest be preserved though the device of a four-mile-long linear park along the ridgetop, a park that would have encompassed the "steep and broken declivities" of High Rock. Unfortunately, those who might have implemented this plan were not endowed with the vision and fortitude to act. So Olmsted's proposal was retired to some musty shelf and would remain there virtually forgotten for nearly a hundred years.

One individual who would not forget was William T. Davis, the memorable native-son naturalist. For three-quarters of a century, almost until his death in 1945, Davis roamed the island's backcountry as no one person ever had before, has since, or will again. His Days Afield on Staten Island, privately published in 1892, witty, dry, and sometimes sad yet dense with scientific information, is still considered a classic; his two-volume work, *Staten Island and Its People* (1930), written in collaboration with Charles W. Leng, remains the most substantial—and readable—local history yet compiled. Toward the end, Davis became increasingly worried about the human pressures on his natural haunts. "Only a few human beings should grow to the square mile," he wrote in one of his voluminous journals. "They commonly are planted too close." For parks, his tastes were closer to Thoreau's than to Olmsted's. "The best park," Davis liked to say, "is certainly a piece of woodland left as Nature arranged it, with a few paths cut through."

Such a piece was Middletown Forest. On a map drawn by Charles Leng in 1896 and lettered by Davis with "ye olde names & nicknames" of landforms and communities, the largest blank space on Staten Island runs from Ocean Terrace south to Egbertville, from the Black Horse Ravine east across Todt Hill to Moravian Brook. And, in their definitive island history, published some forty years later, Leng and Davis would write:

> The crowning glory of Staten Island's topography and scenery is the forest
> that springs from its rich, well-watered soil. . . . [I]n spite of widespread
> cutting during the Revolution for fuel, and continual burning and cut-

ting in recent years, . . . [t]he deep ravines and their adjacent hills, the wetter portions of the swamps, are still well-wooded . . . especially . . . north of the Moravian Cemetery. . . . Irregularity of contour and excessive wetness have saved such places from village development; and there is hope that some at least may ultimately become parklands, for which purpose they are eminently fit.

Davis's fond regard for the Middletown Forest fortunately was shared over the years by most of the people who owned the land. These assorted stewards included the famous Vanderbilt clan, which acquired considerable acreage in the High Rock area in 1843 (the year of Thoreau's errant island rambles), donated some later to the Moravian Cemetery, and passed the rest on from father to son almost for a hundred years. Presumably with the owner's permission, Davis and his colleagues in the Staten Island Bird Club built a rustic cabin in the Vanderbilt woods, north of the cemetery, some time after the turn of the century. The cabin, dismantled about 1926, was located 150 yards from the northern wingtip of the High Rock butterfly, on the shore of Hour-Glass Pond. In 1947, the executors of the Vanderbilt estate sold one parcel adjoining the family mausoleum in the Moravian Cemetery to the Greater New York Council of the Boy Scouts of America. This same land is now a part of High Rock Park.

A second parcel—and the largest within what is High Rock—can be traced to the 1850s and its acquisition by one David Ebbet. In 1855, Ebbet sold one acre to the U.S. government for the construction of a lighthouse. Erected a year later, the New Dorp, or Moravian, Lighthouse guided incoming ships for more than a century, was decommissioned by the Coast Guard in 1964 but soon designated an official landmark by New York City. The Landmarks Preservation Commission described the lighthouse as "unique and vernacular," a "severely-plain . . . clapboard frame building (that) is clearly rugged in character and wind-swept in appearance." The structure today is a private home. The rest of the original tract was acquired by the Boy Scout Council in 1930.

A third parcel consisting of twelve acres was passed on from Delafields to Cocrofts in the nineteenth century and from Cocrofts to Tonkings in the twentieth. The Tonkings operated a chicken farm on the premises and lived in what is now Pouch Laboratory at High

New Dorp (or Moravian) Lighthouse.

Rock. They called their place Mayroyd Farm. Mr. Tonking was in the process of building a new house of fieldstone (the present High Rock administration building) when he died. The house and property were later sold to one Harry Ball, who planned to raise horses instead of chickens but soon decided to raise cash by reselling the farm to the Boy Scouts in 1944.

Of the four other High Rock parcels, two until 1919 had belonged to the Everingham family for a century, and two can be traced back through several ownerships to the estate of the Revolutionary lumberman, Richard Conner. All four, by the mid-1920s, had been acquired and incorporated into a latter-day lordship greater even than Conner's—the Todt Hill domain of architect Ernest Flagg.

Flagg had come to Staten Island in 1897 to assemble this estate and to build, in the Dutch colonial revival style, his monumental home, Stone Court, now St. Charles Seminary, on the opposite side of Todt Hill. He was an innovative architect. In his time, he was responsible for the design of Manhattan's first true skyscraper, the Singer Building; for the Corcoran Art Gallery in Washington, D.C.; and for the buildings of the U.S. Naval Academy at Annapolis, Maryland; but the present landmark status of his own Stone Court, with its Doric columns and complementary gatehouse, is evidence that he will be remembered as well for his bold use of wood forms and fieldstone in executing the design of notable private homes. Flagg died in 1947. Barely two years later, his trustees and executers conveyed by sale to the Boy Scout Council some 100 acres of the estate, including the former Everingham and Conner parcels at High Rock.

In the 1930s, before these final acquisitions, the Scouts had called their original land Short Term Camp, meaning one camped there for one or two nights only. Lean-to's were erected and lodges (one, Buntin Lodge, was totally destroyed by fire in 1943); and before long the camp's directors were counting off 75,000 overnighters a year. The camp attracted the support of wealthy local benefactors: Nathan Ohrbach and Thomas Watson, Jr., and William Pouch. And through the long post-war summers the blue haze of woodsmoke drifted lazily though the treetops, and the clatter of cook-pans echoed across the shallow ponds and down the steep slopes and out among the gravestones of the Moravian greensward. And then, one fine day, on a drawing board in some faraway office, a highway engineer traced a thin blue

Ford Tonking House, the administration building at High Rock Park.

line—two, in fact, since every highway requires a right-of-way—across a map of Todt Hill. The parallel lines curved gracefully, like the blade of a scythe, through the blank spaces of the old Middletown Forest, from Ocean Terrace along the ridgetop and down the tumbling south shoulder to Richmond Brook—the path Thoreau may have taken, that Olmsted must surely have followed to speak so highly of a linear park. And in its sweep the dual line bisected the scout camp, severing some sixty acres from the larger body of the property, lopping off the parcels once owned by Tonking and Vanderbilt and Ebbet and Flagg.

The Richmond Parkway, the people at the drawing boards would call their little blue lines. And, in the board rooms of the Boy Scouts, the men who must react to such decisions shook their heads in sadness and in resignation and, agreeing it would be wise to retain the larger northern element of the camp, voted to sell the smaller part, the lopped-off part, to their distaff colleagues in the Girl Scout Council of Greater New York. The price was $35,000, which may have seemed a lot at the time, for the time was 1951. In any event, the Girl Scout leaders were delighted to have a camp at last within the boundaries of New York City. And I suspect they were delighted as well to hear through the scout grapevine that an energetic camping consultant from Needham, Massachusetts, had just moved with her husband, Horace Moulton, to a white frame house on the eastern escarpment of Todt Hill.

Girl Scouts at a High Rock lean-to.

THE RACE FOR SPACE

Though one hears differing accounts from time to time as to why and how the place came to be called High Rock shortly after the Girl Scouts acquired it, the name most likely was Gretta Moulton's idea, as so many of the lasting ones were. One version of the story, lacking specific attribution to any individual, holds the name to be strictly geomorphic: The land is high and (if you scratch the topsoil) rocky; therefore, High Rock. Another variation accepts the *High* part but adds that the *Rock* is abbreviated tribute to the Rockefeller brothers, whose lump-sum contribution enabled the Girl Scouts to buy the property in the first place. While questioning the validity of neither version, I personally prefer a third: That in Needham, near the Charles River, was a wooded promontory known locally as High Rock; that Gretta Moulton loved the area and simply borrowed its name because it seemed to fit the camp on Staten Island. I cannot swear to this, though others may. I only know that Gretta Moulton came up with enduring ideas and was a person with a fine sense of place.

She had been raised in the scouting tradition at her childhood homes in Waltham and Weston, Massachusetts—short-term camps and day hikes and later, as an adult volunteer, the challenge of making these outdoor exercises as meaningful to a new generation as they had been to her own. For a number of years before the move to Staten Island, she directed the camping program at Cedar Hill, near Belmont, Massachusetts, and was an inveterate traveler to regional "roundups" throughout the Northeast. The Cedar Hill responsibility was especially demanding. Those who were close to her at the time recall she was relieved finally when her husband's work took them both away to New York. But she was not to be inactive for long. Her reputation for getting things done had preceded her to the island, and she was instantly recruited as consultant to the women who had just taken over part of the old Boy Scout Camp on Todt Hill.

One thing that needed getting done was a program to revitalize the land, for the land at High Rock was battered. Boy Scout troops had been tramping and camping across the property for twenty years, and more than a few of their scout masters were the kind of men who are not accustomed to tread lightly in any country. One must also remember that the fabled scout axe was then as much a part of the official scout uniform as the obligatory kerchief and the khaki kneepants. Thus, in the 1950s, one could stroll though certain corridors of the High Rock woodlands wondering where all the saplings had gone, and the brush and the ferns and the grass, and why the compacted earth looked cracked and dry. One could rejoice, however, in the fact that the machismo was now removed to the other side of the tracks, the blue lines of the Richmond Parkway, and that the camping and tramping would henceforth be governed by gentler hands and softer feet.

What's more, the camp's new managers began to rotate the areas selected for intensive use and to reroute some of the more heavily-used trails, so that, by 1960, the old battered corridors were beginning to look green again. And, in all of this, Gretta Moulton was a key participant, involved not only with the immediate needs of the camping program, but with the far more complex aspects of keeping that program in tune with the rhythms of the land itself. In fact, Gretta Moulton and her associates were so absorbed with the rhythms of High Rock that they almost failed to hear the approaching sound of an altogether different kind of music. With the wind in the treetops, they could just barely perceive the faraway jingle of coins.

From the perspective of years, it would be preposterous to suppose now that the notion of selling High Rock should not have flickered then, however dimly, across the minds of people high in the ruling councils of the New York Girl Scouts. Coin is a compelling obsession, even for the most altruistic among us. And so it happened that the notion did indeed cross a mind or two that High Rock might be sold. Especially after a rumor got around that Warren Walker, with property abutting the camp and a pressing family inclination to move away to New Jersey, had been made an offer for his land. Later, in defense of their own decision to sell, some Girl Scout executive would protest that they had "never dreamed" the property could be so valuable. Perhaps Warren Walker had never had such dreams himself. Yet the fact remains that, by 1963, the land the Girl Scouts had acquired twelve years earlier for about $600 an acre was now being valued at some $18,000 per acre—a potential gain on the investment of almost 3,000 percent.

In the fall of that year, a number of camp volunteers from Staten Island and Brooklyn demanded to know what the Girl Scout Council of Greater New York was actually planning to do with High Rock. Were the rumors true, they asked at a meeting of the council's camp committee? Was the council really entertaining the idea of selling High Rock? No comment, but the women were assured that they would soon be hearing from the president of the council's Board of Directors, Mrs. Howard Phipps. And what the volunteers heard from Mrs. Phipps was not much to their liking. What they heard was that Staten Island would soon be changing under the impact of the [Verrazano] Narrows Bridge, that there was an urgent need to be thinking now of developing new camp facilities upstate. Sometime later, other members of the council's hierarchy stated flat-out that High Rock had become more of a liability than an asset—discounting, of course, the cash value of the property. The camp should be closed, reported a Girl Scout director after one visit to High Rock, because "there are bullet holes in one of the buildings . . . and the caretaker reported seeing a peeping tom." Her only interest, the director added, was "to get as much scouting as possible for our girls, and we can get more for them by busing them to our upstate camps."

How *much* more was questioned by the High Rock volunteers. Mrs. Bertil Johnson, the director at Camp High Rock for five years, noted that, for many girls from lower-income families in Brooklyn and Manhattan, the expense of transportation upstate could be prohibitive. The round-trip expense to High Rock then was seventy cents; between the city and Camp Andre Clark near Pleasantville in Westchester County, the fare was two dollars. Moreover, some islanders wondered which was truly higher among the council's priorities—the "girls" or the million-dollar goal of the council's development fund campaign.

So the battle was joined, and for a while it must have seemed a lopsided one at that. Against the prestigious council directors, the

High Rock volunteers at first appeared powerless, parochial, and malcontent. Yet, for all the sputtering, the champions of High Rock had at least two good things going for them. One of these was the voice of a New Conservation, expressed from afar in the natural-beauty pronouncements of Lady Bird Johnson and, closer to home, in the earthy, pragmatic language of landsaving, as preached by the Regional Plan Association and the similarly regional Open Space Action Committee. The other good thing was Gretta Moulton.

In a drastic shift of tactics, Gretta Moulton spread the word that the issue now was not just a scout camp but a priceless natural resource, and she quickly struck on two separate fronts. In Manhattan, she enlisted the support of the Community Council of Greater New York and its Group Work and Recreation Committee, then chaired by Mrs. Leonard Bernheim, a dynamic woman with considerable influence and impeccable credentials in the field of voluntary public service. And, on Staten Island, she proceeded to gain the ear of the one politician whose aid would prove indispensable—Albert V. Maniscalco, the Richmond Borough president.

Even before the High Rock issue had emerged, Maniscalco's vision had taken in the spectacle of subdivisions sprawling up the lower hillsides of the island. And beyond the raw bulldozer cuts he saw the wooded escarpments of Todt and Lighthouse hills—saw them perhaps not with the earthy passion of an Olmsted or Thoreau, but *saw* them nonetheless and understood then how close they were to the approaching blades. In his time in office, Maniscalco christened many public works, but I suspect the names of none of these will in fact or in memory outlast the identity he now imposed on the beleaguered hills. From Emerson Hill down the long ridge, widening through the forest where William Davis had wandered, taking in the scout camps and the parklands of Latourette, Maniscalco saw the vague shape of an opportunity to turn the 'dozers back from the high ground. And what he saw he called the Staten Island Greenbelt.[1] It was a name that would soon be a battle-cry in the fight to save High Rock, a name that for other reasons would come back to haunt both Republicans and Democrats, developers and highway designers for years to come.

By March of 1964, no ambiguity remained as to the Girl Scout Council's intentions for its Staten Island Camp. The intentions were clearly to sell and get out. In June, Mrs. Bernheim and Margaret Wood of the Community Council secured an audience with scout directors and urged that the camp be offered for sale first either to the city or a voluntary agency but not to a developer. The scout council declined to become thus committed. In July, Gretta Moulton's Manhattan forces at the Community Council established an "Ad Hoc Committee on Camp High Rock Site" (later to be shortened to the Subcommittee on Open Lands). Chaired by Mrs. Albert Francke, Jr., the new task force represented a broad range of city interests, its members including Robert Alpern of the Park Association of New York City, John H. Dreasan of the Children's Aid Society, Mrs. Lawrence Farmer of the Group Work and Recreation Committee, Bradford Greene and Robert Hagenhofer of the Staten Island Citizens' Planning Committee, Charles E. Little of the Open Space Action Committee, Mrs. Rowena Shoemaker of Play Schools Association, and State Senator Jerome L. Wilson of the Council on Parks and Playgrounds. Margaret Wood served as secretary to the group, and among its consultants were Melville Daus of the City's Department of Parks, Charles E. Hartsoe of the National Recreation Association, and Edwin Friedman, Alfred Shapiro, and Blanche Wittes of the Department of City Planning. "This was community involvement at its very best," Mrs. Bernheim would recall later. "Though Gretta herself was not officially on the committee, she was the one who pulled it together. She was the catalyst, and she knew how to make other people respond."

From Borough Hall on Staten Island, Albert Maniscalco's response thundered across the front page of the *Staten Island Advance*. The way he saw it, it was "green bucks" against the "Greenbelt," and he vowed to seek a change in the zoning laws to prevent the construction of any high-density housing on the site. And, to support Maniscalco's bid for re-zoning, Gretta Moulton and Bradford Greene, under the banner of yet another ad hoc committee "To Preserve the Greenbelt," widened the community involvement even further by circulating fact-sheets to a score of diverse island organizations. After one joint meeting of the two ad hoc committees, someone in attendance passed a note around the conference table. It stopped at Brad Greene, and he tucked it away in his file. The note, in a hand neither he nor I can trace now after more than a decade, says:

*I am struck by the unusual suitability of a number of names on the . . . committee—Margaret D. **Wood** . . . Grace **DuBois** . . . Bradford M. **Greene** . . . **June** L. **Farmer** . . . I hope this association of names with the outdoors augurs well for the Committee's purpose.*

In time, well enough, but not in September of 1964. That month the Girl Scout Council accepted an offer from New Dorp Gardens, Inc., to purchase High Rock for $1,067,000. The sale was approved, according to the laws governing nonprofit organizations but without public hearings, by a single justice of the Supreme Court in Brooklyn. And the development syndicate, figuring that poured concrete might somehow preempt the possibility of any change in the zoning, moved to the edge of the camp (having already purchased the adjacent Walker tract as well) and proceeded to lay the foundations for garden apartments. The saga of High Rock, noted urban affairs writer Jerome Zukosky in *The New York Herald-Tribune* in December, was beginning to sound like "The Perils of Pauline."

That High Rock, like Pauline, would be snatched from the villain's clutches in the final frames of the show was not the kind of ending too many people were betting on. Even Maniscalco knew that rezoning to exclude garden apartments—an action adopted in December by the City Planning Commission and the Board of Estimate—would not truly save the land, but simply encourage the alternative of single-family homes (a touch, Zukosky noted dourly, not of wildness but of Westchester). So, at best, the rezoning was a holding action, a stall. But it borrowed the time that Gretta Moulton and Maniscalco and the planning commissioners, notably Greenbelt-booster Elinor Guggenheimer, would need to negotiate the only lasting solution—the acquisition of High Rock as a city park. And in those days, when one was talking about a million-dollar park, one did not go to Parks Commissioner Newbold Morris. One went to Morris's mentor, to the very top, to the master builder, to power broker, the parkland entrepreneur himself. One went, in short, to Robert Moses.[2]

It is perhaps convenient now for some who were involved at the time to forget the role that Robert Moses played in the saving of High Rock. Perspectives do change, as do the bases of power. Yet no rearrangement of perspective or power can change the fact that Moses was the man with the key to the money-box, even though that box rested under the elbow of Laurance Rockefeller, the governor's brother and then Chairman of the New York State Council of Parks. Accounts vary as to the details of Moses's involvement, except in one aspect: He wanted High Rock badly, wanted it as he had once wanted (and lost) the nearby golf course of the Richmond County Country Club. Moses, the incurable stringer of beads to any convenient necklace, wanted High Rock for the very simple reason that it already dangled from the thin blue lines of the Richmond Parkway.

The money in the box amounted to about $8,000,000, a residue of state recreation bond-issue funds already allocated to upstate cities but unused. Moses knew he could get about $900,000 from the fund, about three-quarters of what it would cost to acquire High Rock from the developer, if the city would ante up the remaining dollars. Albert Maniscalco recalls that Moses personally "laid it on the line." Moses told him, said Maniscalco, that the city had to commit its share first and that "then Moses would get the big money from Rockefeller." According to Maniscalco:

> *I had to hustle, believe me. I said to the other borough presidents, 'If we let this go by default, we should hang our heads.' Well, they'd hardly heard of High Rock. I had to take a couple of them up there to show them what it was really like. They could hardly believe it. . . . So, sure. We found the dough in the capital budget, and that clinched everything. . . . And—I'll never forget it—the day after the word got out that High Rock was saved, who comes into my office but Mrs. Moulton. She comes over to me and throws her arms around me. Just like that. And you know what? So help me, I think there were tears in her eyes.*

On April 4, 1965, the City of New York filed a notice of the pendancy of a condemnation proceeding to acquire sixty-two acres at High Rock for public purposes. The award granted by the court to the owners of the property, New Dorp Gardens, Inc., was $1,260,000. (The eleven-acre Walker tract would be acquired later that year for $295,000.) And on July 7 High Rock was dedicated officially as parkland, albeit not the kind of parkland to which either Newbold Morris or Robert Moses might have been accustomed, as we shall presently see. Gretta Moulton was there for the ribbon-cutting, as were President Louis Miller and Executive Director George O. Pratt, Jr., of the

Walker Pond.

Staten Island Institute of Arts and Sciences, which would soon be playing a key role itself in the transformation of a scout camp into a conservation center. And one should not overlook the presence of Albert V. Maniscalco, beaming as he sliced the ribbon. There were no formal speeches, although Maniscalco later spoke to a reporter from the *Staten Island Advance*. It was a fine occasion, he told the newsman, a splendid reminder of our "moral duty to see that such places which nature has so beautifully blessed are protected from the hammers and axes of the seekers of the fast dollar." And with that the Perils of High Rock seemed to be over. But, in fact, they had only begun.

*(Left to right) Albert V. Maniscalco, Governor Nelson A. Rockefeller,
and George D. Pratt, Jr., from a photograph in the* Staten Island Advance.

GETTING FROM HERE TO THERE

To what extent the prospects of the Richmond Parkway may have skulked across the peripheral visions of High Rock's saviors in the summer and fall of 1965 I do not pretend to know, nor care much either. If it matters at all now, the likeliest truth is that perceptions of peril were dulled in the rosy afterglow of the July 7th ribbon-cutting; that there would soon enough be other things to worry about (namely, securing an adequate operating budget for the park); that, whatever one's personal sense of dismay might have been, there was no precedent at the time for any response to the parkway other than the traditional mute resignation. After all, it was a *Robert Moses* project, and Moses wanted it badly. Even Albert Maniscalco wanted it. The cartographers at Hagstrom's surely wanted it, for they had already drawn the parkway in place on the map of Richmond County along with the phantom subdivisions. In just a few months, one could assume that the bulldozers would be making monockong on the right-of-way. Yet, within that critical period remaining before the actual start of construction, such assumptions would be shattered by a random combination of circumstances. The Richmond Parkway, or rather the section through the Staten Island Greenbelt, would indeed be challenged—challenged so effectively that now, a full decade later, no one has the foggiest idea as to where or when or even whether the road might be built.

The first circumstance was the map. It was spread across a table in the graphics-design office of Robert Hagenhofer, Chairman of the Staten Island Citizens Planning Committee and former member of the Ad Hoc Committee on Camp High Rock Site. Hagenhofer had a visitor: Bradford Greene, also of the two committees, a landscape architect, and author of the "Greenbelt" paper recently published in *The New*

Bulletin. Greene was pointing a pencil at the map. The tip was on High Rock. Hagenhofer was looking at a point just north of the pencil, where the parallel lines of the Richmond Parkway curved though the phantom subdivisions, through what Greene and Maniscalco had been calling the Greenbelt.

"Some Greenbelt," said Hagenhofer. "A quarter of it's highway."

"Or will be," Greene added.

Hagenhofer said he wasn't so sure about that. "I think," he said, "that we'd better start asking some tough questions . . . ."

The second circumstance was the November 8, 1965, Staten Island appearance of Governor Nelson Rockefeller, come to hobnob with his southern constituents and, incidentally, to see for himself this place which he and his brother, Laurance, and Bob Moses had helped to snatch from the scythe of the reaper. The governor was delighted with High Rock and praised its natural beauty. And, in the audience, Brad Greene and Alan Oser, another planning committee strategist, nudged Hagenhofer to his feet to ask the first tough question. "Mister Governor," said Hagenhofer, "it is proposed that a state highway be built immediately adjacent to this beautiful area so many of us here have worked so hard to save." Hagenhofer paused, his arm outstretched, an accusing finger pointing toward the parkway right-of-way. "And, Mister Governor," he went on, "my question is—is there any good reason why a road should be built though these woods?"

The governor had no good reason at the moment. It was a question, he said, for Burch McMorran, the state superintendent of public works. Later, Burch McMorran said it was a question for his district engineer in Babylon, Long Island. So the citizen-planners went to Babylon; but in Babylon they learned that their question was really for Bob Moses of the Triborough Bridge and Tunnel Authority on Randall's Island. By this time, the islanders were beginning to suspect there was no good reason why the road had to be built through the Greenbelt's woods adjoining High Rock. In December 1965, they released a position paper urging that the highway be shifted to the west of High Rock and the Boy Scout Camp and pointed out to Moses and McMorran their conviction that, if built as originally planned, the Richmond Parkway would destroy forever the wild charm of the area.

The third crucial circumstance was the response this position paper elicited from Moses and the public works engineers. Instead of ignoring it altogether as the braying of a pack of amateurs with no good standing, Moses chose to give the paper public credence by attacking it. "Impractical and visionary," said Moses sternly of the planning committee's alternate route—a response that *The New York Times*, lately disenchanted with its hero, chidingly characterized in an editorial as Moses's "favorite thunder." Thus, with only nine typewritten pages and one sketch-map, the planning committee had acquired what Moses might otherwise have denied them—the stature of a powerful professional adversary.

And the fourth circumstance, perhaps the most critical of all, was the mayoral election of John V. Lindsay, who moved into City Hall less than thirty-six hours after the lame-duck Robert Ferdinand Wagner signed an order authorizing the letting of bids for construction of the Richmond Parkway, as originally planned.

I must tread carefully now across the shards of subsequent events, for I was a participant in some, a close observer in others, and at all times a cantankerous partisan in the cause of removing the Richmond Parkway from the precincts of High Rock and the Staten Island Greenbelt. Therefore, I can promise no great measure of objectivity in reviewing those events, except to say in fairness that there are neither heroes nor villains in this episode but, rather, two very different kinds of people with sharply contrasting perceptions and styles and tastes. I mean there were and are those who perceive the Greenbelt much as our Pilgrim forebears must have viewed the dark and satanic forests of New England—as a place for wild savages, at once inaccessible and to be avoided; as fallow soil, unclaimed property, wasted and unholy land. I mean there were and are people who actually regard the Greenbelt as a fire hazard (and the parkway an effective fire-break); who truly feel (as Robert Moses said *he* did on June 29, 1967) that preserving the Greenbelt as a natural area might somehow turn it into "the most dangerous place in New York City" and who, like Moses, cannot conceive of any valid form of outdoor recreation unless it is played out within earshot of moving pistons. Yes, there are really people like that. Sincere people. They are alive and well not only on Staten Island, but in Babylon and Albany and even in Manhattan.

The other kind of people were and are those with a softer view of the Greenbelt, the kind who are not threatened by voids on a map, unpaved paths, or blissful silence; indeed, the kind who actually *appreciate* such things. To be sure, because of the nature of our society, these people also drive automobiles; and at no time have any of them denied the need for a better way of getting an automobile from here to there or, rather, from the Staten Island Expressway to the Outerbridge Crossing. In fact, over the years, some of these people demonstrated a number of ways to get an automobile from here to there without obliterating a quarter of the Greenbelt in the process. But, every time, someone from the other side would find a reason why it couldn't be done. And why couldn't it be done? Why, because it was impractical and visionary.

In his time as Mayor of New York City, John V. Lindsay was among the impractical visionaries. In fact, he was surrounded by them. There was City Planning Commissioner Elinor Guggenheimer, for one, a holdover from the Wagner days. "Ellie," everyone called her on that frigid day in January 1966 as she led the first band of Greenbelt hikers up Helena Road and into the snowy woods toward High Rock. And there was William Ballard, the planning commission's chairman who first recognized the wisdom of rerouting the parkway far to the west of the Greenbelt; and his successor, Donald Elliot, who continued the effort in that direction; and Arthur Palmer, the transportation czar who usurped Moses's seat of power; and Thomas P. F. Hoving, the charismatic parks administrator who, in tasseled stocking-cap and knickers, led a High Rock hike or two himself and preached the Greenbelt gospel across the nation; and, later, August Heckscher, who thought of High Rock as the most "enchanted" gem in his entire public domain ("Augie," everyone called him that balmy January day in 1968 as he led another band across the thawing bottoms of Bucks Hollow, side by side with the visiting archdruid, David Brower, and Heckscher's young aide, Roy Neuberger); and Holt Meyer, the mayor's embattled Staten Island development director, who grinningly endured the local scorn of the Lindsay-baiters; and Meyer's colleague, the late Sam Joroff, who, perhaps more than anyone else in a critical staff position at the time, fully understood the intrinsic value of untrammeled land and of natural processes functioning, uninterrupted, in the city of man. For all its tactical errors, oversights, and

Birds of High Rock.

indecisions, it was a spirited gang—while it lasted. And the regrettable probability is that, in New York City, we shall never be privileged to see the exact likes of it again.

Early in 1966, Lindsay rescinded Wagner's construction consent (illegally, it was later determined in court) and retained a consulting firm to analyze a number of alternate parkway routes.[1] Meanwhile, Hagenhofer and Greene, along with attorneys Terence Benbow and the late Frank Duffy, were busy broadening the Citizens Planning Committee's base of support. Among the first organizations to join the fray were the Scenic Hudson Preservation Conference and the National Audubon Society (which had just completed a site survey of High Rock under a grant from the American Conservation Association). Other allies soon included the Park Association of New York City and the Council for Parks & Playgrounds (now merged as The

Turtles.

Parks Council), the prestigious Municipal Art Society of New York, the Community Council of Greater New York, the New York-New Jersey Trail Conference, the Appalachian Mountain Club, the New York Chapter of the American Institute of Architects, the New York Board of Trade (not to be confused with any chamber of commerce), the Women's City Club, and the Sierra Club, whose founding father, John Muir, had been among the first to articulate for laymen the basic premise of ecology: "When we try to pick out anything by itself, we find it hitched to everything else in the universe." On the home front, the Greenbelt coalition was bolstered by the Todt Hill and Lighthouse Hill civic associations and by a cadre of conservation commandos calling themselves the Staten Island Greenbelt-Natural Areas League (SIGNAL), among whose founding members were several individuals who then or later would be intimately involved in the on-going affairs of High Rock—Gretta Moulton and Elizabeth Seder and Doris Barlow and Harry Betros and Wesley Truesdell.

One of the first goals of SIGNAL and the Citizens Planning Committee was to find a positive nonhighway use for the acquired right-of-way of the Original Route, should they be so lucky as to succeed in removing the proposed highway from the Greenbelt. And they found a use, with the help of Brad Green's research, in Frederick Law Olmsted's 1871 report for the Staten Island Improvement Commission:

> *In the case of Staten Island (Olmsted had written), it would be simple plan to form a park . . . four miles in length. . . . It would occupy a moderately central position and turn to good use a large extent of land. . . . This ridge extends from the Fresh Kills near Richmond to Stapleton, but while its altitude is melted away in gentle slopes to the northward . . . permitting in that quarter the greatest freedom in the location of roads, it descends toward the sea on the south in steep and broken declivities, totally unsuited, not to say impracticable, for roads for rapid travel.*

Seizing on this century-old plan, the Greenbelt advocates went to their typewriters and drafting tables, and in August of 1966, in the Central Park Arsenal office of Thomas Hoving, issued a slick, sixteen-page brochure entitled, *The Olmsted Trailway: A Proposal for Outdoor Recreation in the Staten Island Greenbelt.* The brochure noted U.S. Interior Secretary Stewart Udall's recent mandate to establish a nationwide system of hiking trails, especially near urban centers, and went on to describe the opportunities for developing—in lieu of a parkway—a 4.7-mile linear park along the right-of-way of the Original Route, with foot-, bike-, and bridle-paths threading the woodland corridor from the Community College in Sunnyside south past High Rock to the Richmondtown Restoration. Hoving hailed it as "a bold and imaginative plan." The pilgrims on the other side called it impractical and visionary.

And on it went, proposals and counter-proposals, allegations and denials, debates, diatribes, public hearings, private whispers. And no action. No highway. No trailway. Only words. Continually, the *Staten Island Advance* pleaded editorially for some kind of compromise. But how could there be compromise between two intellectually, emotionally, and—one regrets to add—politically polarized parties, one perceiving the Greenbelt as a vehicular corridor, the other viewing it as the last great reservoir of sylvan open space in New York City?

So the days dwindled down to a precious few, as did the available options for an alternate parkway route. For as it happened—as Lindsay and Rockefeller, Palmer and McMorran and Moses and various federal highway panjandrums were jockeying for position—some enterprising developers moved bulldozers to the west flank of the Greenbelt and proceeded to build within and across the proposed Alternate Four right-of-way a solid wall of new homes. *Fait accompli.* By 1970, the Lindsay side was wearing down. Finally, with reluctance, Lindsay settled for Alternate Six, which is simply the Original Route with a bulge in it and, therefore, unacceptable to the Greenbelt coalition (now know as the Greenbelt Emergency Conference).

And then Lindsay was gone. His successor, Abraham Beame, soon appointed a task force to review the Richmond Parkway options once again. The group, strangely lacking any appointed representative of the Greenbelt Conference, seemed at first to be sticking with Six. More recently, there have been indications of a switch—to the Original Route.

Yet High Rock prevails. Some optimists say it will not matter much for High Rock if the parkway pushes though as Moses first planned it, straight across the north wingtip of the butterfly, gouging deeply into the ridge between Flagg Pond at the Boy Scout Camp and the loosestrife swamp. Some say that the sound of traffic will be muffled by the trees—the few that will be left after site preparation. Some, believing that automobile air pollution ended with the advent of the catalytic converter, dismiss more recent fears that unconverted oxides of nitrogen will waft across the park on prevailing westerlies and at intolerable ambient levels, and some go so far as to say that the High Rock experience might actually benefit from the parkway presence, inasmuch as the park's urban visitors will then feel more "at home" in the woods within sound and smell of moving cars—and, indeed, if one is sitting on that glacial erratic at the far end of the swamp, within sight of cars, too.

But, as I was saying, it is all a matter of taste and perception. For my own part, I do not see High Rock withering on the vine should the Original Route proceed. Nor do I see it blooming. I see it sort of hunkering there, thin and gray around the edges, like any other roadside park in America; a bland kind of place for bland kinds of tastes. Yet for a number of reasons, most of them having to do with the law,

I doubt that it will ever happen that way. If I had to call it one way or another, I'd guess that, at some point in the future when we try to pick out High Rock by itself, we'll find it hitched to almost every good thing in the universe. And I don't mean four concrete lanes and one median strip. I mean wind and weather and rock and humus, and plants succeeding, and tall trees dying of old age. And receptive, perceptive people walking softly and unhurriedly though the woods, looking for the kind of human experience that only an undisturbed High Rock can help them discover.

Gretta Moulton and two colleagues hiking at High Rock.

MORE PERILS, MORE FRIENDS

If High Rock's first six years in the public domain were perilous ones—and clearly they were—the incentive for nail-biting was not the Richmond Parkway alone. Two immediate problems loomed even larger: the perennial scurry for operating funds and the recurring visions of well-meaning folk and misguided bureaucrats, who saw in the open lands there an opportunity to fulfill their wildest capital-intensive dreams. Some people just have to think *BIG*.

The first big idea was advanced before High Rock had been dedicated as parkland; so that, perhaps, the purveyor of the brainstorm should be forgiven his sin, for he knew not what he said when he said that High Rock would make a dandy detention facility for wayward females. He was a state official, the man who said this, and charity obliges me to forget his name. In any event, he undoubtedly was much taken with the fact that The Rock had been female turf for some time and that, if it was good enough for Girl Scouts, it would be even better for prostitutes and shop-lifters (the Women's House of Detention in Greenwich Village then being, administratively and structurally, something of a house of ill-repute itself). Fortunately, the official's brilliant scheme was never taken seriously. High Rock, someone opined at the time, was better suited to growing trees than mandatory sentences.

Then, for a while, the question became: What kind of trees? There were a number of suggestions, but the most memorable was advanced by a former Staten Island councilman, who briefly and with zeal promoted the conversation of High Rock into a "botanical garden" with "ample" parking for the throngs arriving by way of the Richmond Parkway. The councilman, being no botanist himself, did not specify which exotic species should be planted to replace the native oaks and sweetgums. Instead, his public utterances only amplified on ample parking. And no one took him very seriously either.

Yet over the years, ironically, threats to the park's natural integrity have also been initiated—or at least implied—not only by naïve outsiders, but by the very stewards of the place itself. In 1965, for example, before High Rock's role as a nature conservation center had been fully developed, the top spot on any conservationist's New York enemies list must surely have been occupied by Newbold Morris and his zealous tree-pruners in the Department of Parks. Morris had quite a reputation in those days for attempting to replicate the Sheep Meadow throughout the entire parks system, and one did not have to search far afield to find examples of his pruner's work. On Staten Island, the classic showcase was Von Briesen Park, once a splendid tangle of diverse shrubs, a fine patch of wild overlooking the Narrows, and one of the most ecologically stable small-bird sanctuaries in the city—but now a brushless, pruned and manicured, formal sort of place where only a few older trees and the view remain intact. To what end? Why, to make it *safe*; to discourage muggers and rapists and peeping toms; or, in the unforgettable parlance of Southeast Asia, to destroy it in order to save it. So it goes.

And so, understandably enough, a thinking person figured that the same fate might well befall High Rock. An associate of Gretta Moulton recalls her telling of her Parks Department "nightmares" in the spring of '65. "She kept having these visions," he said, "of Parks Department trucks piled high with power saws and rotor-tillers and benches and picnic tables and bleachers, poised at the gates of High Rock, waiting to blitz the place as soon as the ribbon was cut." Having saved High Rock from the developer, Gretta Moulton would say, it had now become necessary to save the park from *Parks*. (And, a few years later, it would become necessary for the Staten Island Institute of Arts and Sciences, the Park's co-steward at High Rock, to save a part of the place from its own desperate need for new space beyond cramped and scattered quarters in St. George.[1])

In the long and short of it, Gretta Moulton's "nightmares" may have been the happiest turn for High Rock—apart from its public acquisition—since William Howe's grenadiers packed up their axes and sailed away from the stumps on Todt Hill. Her fear that the forest would be vandalized by men with rakes and pruning shears soon spread to others on the Community Council's Subcommittee on Open Lands; and, in the months between assurance of acquisition and formal dedication of the park in July, that committee began to explore a number of alternate uses for the land.

At first, family camping figured among the leading contenders. It seemed a logical extension of the land's prior use but also posed certain administrative problems, which some committee members viewed as insurmountable. Day camping was also discussed. June Farmer, who at the time was the director of day camp programs for the City Health Department, saw High Rock functioning as a demonstration training center for summer counselors. Yet this plan also met with resistance. June Farmer recalls that Gretta Moulton was not much taken with it. "I could tell," recalls Mrs. Farmer, "that Gretta was thinking of something else."

As it turned out, she was thinking of the Staten Island Institute of Arts and Sciences and of a program of nature study that would justify the preservation of High Rock in its current natural and unpruned state. The institute's credentials for undertaking such a task were almost perfect. Offspring of the old Natural Science Association and forum over the years for such notable Island naturalists as Davis, Hollick, Louis Gratacap, and Howard Cleaves, the institute was already a fountainhead of nature lore and scholarly research in the earth sciences. What's more, it had for many years administered (and continues to administer) a nature program at another city park, the William T. Davis Wildlife Refuge near Travis. And the institute's executive director, George O. Pratt, Jr., was (and is) known widely as a man with a deep personal commitment to the environmental ethic, the kind of man whose lasting perception of High Rock would remain closer to Davis's Middletown Forest than to Morris's Sheep Meadow. "Can you get a program started up there by the end of July?" Gretta Moulton asked George Pratt one day. Pratt said he could but added that they would need the full blessing of Newbold Morris.

Seven days before the ribbon cutting, Morris conveyed his blessing to Pratt in a letter of understanding. "The Institute," Morris wrote, "will assume full responsibility and control for the execution of a program covering the various aspects of a nature study and conservation center on this property." The letter further called for establishment of a High Rock Development Committee, representative of the Parks and Recreation Department, the Staten Island Institute of Arts and Sciences, the Community Council, "and other appropriate civic organizations and interested citizens," and Morris charged the committee with responsibility for "developing a long-range plan for future Operations. . . ." The matter of money was barely mentioned.

From the beginning, money has always been at the brittle edge of the High Rock cliff-hangers, holding programs high above the yawning abyss yet threatening at any moment to crumble away, like eroded serpentine, and plunge the place to a mournful end on the scree of public and private indifference. And always (so far), somehow, at the very last moment, the edge has held. It was even that way the first time around with Title III.

Pratt had seen it coming the first summer at High Rock—come November, no funds. But his eyes were also on Washington then, and some encouraging things were beginning to happen that way. Lady Bird Johnson was sounding like Henry Thoreau. Lyndon Johnson was convening a White House Conference on Natural Beauty. And at the U.S. Office of Education there was something new called Title III. It was a huge pile of federal money, and it was up for grabs by institutions qualified to teach the elementary school children of America, among other things, what Mrs. Johnson was really talking about. "Outdoor education," the federal grants people called one of their new programmatic interests. Pratt called it good fortune and proceeded to apply for a piece of the action.

As anyone with even a remote comprehension of the federal bureaucracy might suspect, grant applications can be burdensome affairs. They take time and a great deal of attention to petty detail. Pratt's application took so much time in November of 1965 that, on the night before the last-chance deadline to file, he found himself with his administrative assistant, Elsie Verkuil, on the top floor of the Board of Education building at 110 Livingston Street, Brooklyn, racing the clock to complete the massive document in time for the board's noon pouch to the Office of Education in Washington. *Cliff-hanger! Distress! Shades of Pauline!* Pratt sat surrounded by windrows of quadruplicate forms. Mrs. Verkuil sat at an adding machine, checking the math. Suddenly, the machine went juiceless. Dead. The overhead lights flickered and failed. "Wouldn't you know it would happen to us?" recalls Mrs. Verkuil. "It was the night of the Great Blackout, and we hardly had a match between us." In the dark, they gathered up the papers and groped their way down to the street. "It took forever to get back to Staten Island," says Mrs. Verkuil. "But at least the lights were on when we got there." In the morning, Pratt prevailed on several friendly St. George businessmen to run off the requisite fifty copies of the application, hopped in his car, and floored it for Brooklyn. "And we made it," Pratt says. "With three minutes to spare." He also made something else, for High Rock: $266,557 in Title III funds spread over the remainder of the fiscal year and throughout the two following, up to June 30, 1968.

And then, inevitably—back to the edge. Ethel Dicke remembers it vividly, as well she should, having been though all of the cliff-hangers from the beginning. Ethel Dicke was the assistant to the director at High Rock. In mid-June 1968, she was about to become the former assistant to the former director. Title III was running out. The Ford Foundation, at the urging of Bethuel M. Webster (a Ford trustee and law associate of John V. Lindsay), had pledged $65,000 to help continue the program for another year, but so far the city had not seen fit to match that commitment. There were budget problems at City Hall and the Arsenal. And so Ethel Dicke and George Pratt and other staffers assembled one day at the old stone house that serves at High Rock's headquarters. "It was a wake," says Ethel Dicke. "Time was running out on us. We feared we'd be finished on the first of July." Expecting that, Mrs. Dicke was determined to keep busy. She began packing the High Rock library into boxes that would be shipped to the Board of Education when the program shut down. Then the phone rang. The call was for Pratt. "I'll never forget the look on his face when he came away from the phone," says Mrs. Dicke. "Or what he said." What he said was: "We're in." The city council had just approved a $65,000 line-item to match the grant from Ford. "So, of course," says Mrs. Dicke, "there was only one thing to do. We unpacked the books."

And yet again to the edge: city budget hearings, 1969. This time around, High Rock was seeking full public funding. This one, Elsie Verkuil remembers. "We followed the Metropolitan Museum of Art. We always follow the Met. And that's a hard act to follow. . . . Of course, it looked rough. It always looks rough at budget time. Well, we figured, maybe we should put on an act ourselves. So we came with jars of honey from the hives at High Rock, and we passed them out at the hearing, and the reporters loved it." The city council apparently appreciated the gesture as well, for High Rock shortly thereafter received full funding for yet another year.

Somewhere back a way, I avowed there were no heroes in this piece; alas, that will have to go down as a hollow promise, for personal memory and the scrapbooks of High Rock are filled with the names of innumerable heroes who contributed hugely in ways that cannot be measured by dollars and cents. I mean the people who helped to make High Rock what it is today, each one laying on his or her own measure of understanding and joy and, yes, even passion for the place, through all the cliff-hanging episodes, from the bottom up, until the foundations of the High Rock idea were staunch enough to match the imagery of the High Rock name.

Names . . . such as Phillip J. Brown, the park's pilot director who guided the unproven program through its first year of trial and error. And Charlotte DuBois, who succeeded Brown and shared with the staff insights gleaned from her experience at nature centers in North Carolina and Ohio. And Harry Betros, the biology teacher who followed Ms. DuBois as education director. It was Betros, his predecessors, and their staffs who erected the frame-work of High Rock's education program and hammered it lastingly in place. And one must not forget Edwin Rundlett, the gentle horticulturist and gardening columnist for the *Staten Island Advance*, marking the first nature trails and writing the self-guiding pamphlets to go with them (and then waging total and ungentle war on the exotic pestiferous ailanthus—the *Tree of Heaven?*—which threatened to choke out the native stock). And Mathilde Weingartner, the institute's science curator, who helped train volunteer guides for the High Rock trails (and, indeed, the guides themselves). And there was Cynthia Jacobson, who worked early and hard to enlist the support of the Island's Federated Garden Clubs (which would later sponsor the development at High Rock of a Garden for the Blind, complete with descriptive signs in Braille). And later, too, Ms. Jacobson would direct the first effort to export the High Rock idea to the island's centers of higher education, and she would spearhead as well a campaign to halt

Garden for the Blind.

the city's irresponsible disposal of "surplus" DDT in the Fresh Kills Landfill. No list, however incomplete, should omit mention of the Men's Garden Club of Staten Island and the Staten Island Federation of Sportsmen's Clubs, both of which pitched in generously with volunteer time and money to complete a number of early projects.

And then Friends of High Rock, conceived by Gretta Moulton in 1969 and dedicated to the proposition that all institutions are created unequal and in direct proportion to the strength of their grassroots constituencies. Alison Mitchell and Elizabeth Seder headed that effort (and, later, Roberta Braisted). Within a year of its inception, Friends of High Rock counted some 500 dues-paying members and was by far the largest environmental organization on Staten Island.

Now it was 1970, but fiscal muscle and political clout were not the only things on Gretta Moulton's mind. She was chairperson still of the High Rock Development Committee, the long-range planning group mandated five years earlier by Newbold Morris. And the long-range planning, despite various studies by outside consultants, was getting nowhere. As land-use specialist Charles E. Little (formerly of the Open Space Action Committee) noted in his own consulting report for High Rock that year: "It is not necessary to re-invent the wheel." The important thing, said Little, was for High Rock to retain an administrative executive (inasmuch as George Pratt was largely tied to his St. George museum duties and Harry Betros was busy directing the on-going educational program). And, with an administrator undistracted by other duties, Little suggested, High Rock might begin to function not only as a place for interpretive nature programs, but "as a kind of symbolic center, a nucleus with vectors of energy radiating to every aspect of the environmental challenge confronting New York City."

And there undoubtedly was something else on Gretta Moulton's mind that year: her personal health. She never spoke of it, but the diagnosis was cancer.

Gretta Moulton died on November 18, 1971. She was sixty. A memorial service was held three days later in the old Girl Scout council ring, across the winding blacktop from the staunch stone house that Tonking built. Just inside the front door of that house, in the foyer and riveted to the stone itself, is a bronze plaque designating High Rock as a National Environmental Education Landmark. The embossed message reads:

> *This site possesses distinctive values in revealing significant natural and cultural processes through effective environmental education programs.*

Gretta Moulton lived to accept that landmark designation in person, but she never saw the plaque. It arrived after she was gone. Three months earlier, however, she had seen—and interviewed—the man who would be High Rock's new administrative director, Elliot Willensky, had asked him what he felt his most difficult challenge at High Rock might be. And I am told by others who were present that her eyes lit up when he said that the challenge would be to open High Rock even wider to the public in a way that would not destroy the resource. "But it should always be," Willensky had added, "a place where people come to *enjoy* as well as to learn." For Gretta Moulton, I suspect, hearing that might have been even better than a landmark designation.

Among the 200 or more people who attended the memorial service was a High Rock staffer with a very special memory. She was standing beyond the council ring under a sere autumnal sweetgum tree. Star-shaped leaves were falling at her feet. And what she remembered was one of her last conversations with Gretta Moulton three or four days before the woman's death. The staffer had been at her desk in the stone house; outside—sunbather's sky, wind in the treetops, the warmth of Indian summer. A phone call. From Gretta.

"What are you doing in there?"

"I'm working," said the staffer.

"I know that," said Gretta Moulton. "But it's a nice day at High Rock. Go outdoors and enjoy your life."

REACH-OUT

In recent years, High Rock has come to mean far more than a place in the woods or a fine patch of wild—not that patch or place isn't *meaning* enough. But, today, in a way it never had a chance to be during perilous early times, High Rock is an idea as well, an idea expressed in a diversity of programs reaching out to people of all ages on Staten Island and throughout the metropolitan area. Not everyone has yet been reached. "O, that High Rock," a friend remarked in innocence not long ago. "That's the wildlife refuge on Todt Hill." I did not bother to correct the man's semantics. Instead, borrowing shamelessly from Wallace Stegner, I replied: "Yes, the one where *we* are the wildlife."

As for what actually goes on at High Rock and from High Rock, I would guess that part of any innocent public confusion might well be attributed to the proper name of the place itself. On the surface of it, would seem a bit of a contradiction, for, in popular parlance as well as in practice, a park is for recreation while a conservation center connotes uses considerably more restrained. Yet High Rock is and must be both. And therein lies its greatest challenge: to provide, without loss or waste of the physical resource itself, the opportunity for people to discover joy and significance in the relatedness of all things hitched together under the roof of the house of life, in that domicile of air, water, soil, and fire we happen to call our Total Environment.

The learning process at High Rock is, of course, most visible in the elementary and secondary education program first funded by Title III in 1966. Every year since then, more than 25,000 students have been accommodated at High Rock by advance reservation. Each visiting class arrives by bus for an hour-and-a-half session in one of the center's laboratory classrooms and on the trails; and to each is assigned a naturalist-instructor and two guides. Three naturalist-instructors figured prominently in this program in recent years: Mildred Becker, on "loan" from the New York City Board of Education; Olivia Hansen, who has been a key figure in summer-camp leadership training programs and in interpretive work with the handicapped; and Rudolf Lindenfeld, a white-haired Petrarchan sonneteer (*Ode to a Wildflower*) whose approach to nature itself is poetic. "Mr. Lindenfeld," wrote one grateful Queens teacher, "held us all spellbound. . . . The children claim this trip was the best they ever had, even though it was educational."

In the beginning, there was some difficulty relating what essentially was a traditional nature-appreciation concept to an audience frequently composed of urban children. A Staten Island student might feel at home among the center's tall trees, but that would not always be the case for the visitor from Bensonhurst or the South Bronx. And on the trail, influenced perhaps by the resolute "don't-touch" theories then in vogue at certain venerable and exurban nature centers, High Rock guides sometimes innocently created an artificial barrier between their subject and their charges, as if the pressure of one tiny hand against the bark of one tall tree might somehow and forever upset the balance of nature. Yet over time, without relaxing its mandate to conserve the resource ("Take nothing away, leave footprints"), High Rock staffers have evolved a more open-ended approach in which students are encouraged to discover for themselves, through their own senses if they can, the lessons that nature in all seasons stands mutely prepared to impart. This approach also seeks to use High Rock not as an isolated arena for indigenous show-and-tell, but as a kind of model to remind the visitor of lessons yet to be learned—and actions yet to be taken—in his or her own community, no matter how tame the landscape or how scrawny the trees.

Similarly, an effort has been made from the beginning to provide the kind of summer programs that assure High Rock's year-round use as an educational center. Among the first of these was a YMCA day-camp program offering guided, trailside nature interpretation and a Board of Education program, "Science in the Parks," for vacationing school children.

Less visible, perhaps, though no less important has been High Rock's effort to extend its educational program beyond its own campus and into the classrooms of Staten Island (a move pioneered by Board of Education Science Curriculum Coordinator Margaret Beyer). For example, when inclement weather begins to slow the pace of scheduled on-site classes, High Rock instructors arrange to visit the schools directly, thereby avoiding a waste of human resources while, not so incidentally, reaching more children than could actually be accommodated at the center in the same period of time. High Rock has also developed a cooperative program with Richmond College (a unit of the City University of New York), in which instructors from the center have sought to share their knowledge and experience with student-teachers. This program likewise eschews the idea that High Rock is the only place for the proper study of environment; instead, student-teachers are encouraged to use local resources in the vicinity of the school to which they have been assigned.

For all its distinctive good work in the field of environmental education, High Rock has been moving of late in some new and different directions largely charted by Elliot Willensky, the director from 1971 to 1976. Willensky was no old-school-tie preservationist, rushing about with a butterfly net and shouting "Don't touch" at the drop of an oak leaf. He is an urban man, an architect by profession, and for several years before coming to High Rock he was August Hecksher's deputy administrator for development in Parks, Recreation and Cultural Affairs, the man in charge of planning that agency's capital expenditures. Considering the pedigree, one would think Elliot Willensky might have rushed about High Rock with a sliderule, shouting instructions at contractors. But he was not doing that either. He was sitting in his office in the house that Tonking built, remembering how, under Heckscher, it was not the development of new public works that had fascinated him but rather the agency's established assets: the "rich storehouse of undeveloped land," he called it, "the wilder innards of Alley Pond and Van Cordlandt and Inwood and Jamaica Bay" (he had not then seen High Rock), and the city's great cultural institutions, supported by the agency and dedicated to the proposition that the public shall be served. "And in High Rock," said Willensky, "I saw that rare and wonderful combination—a priceless natural resource and a cultural institution with the capacity to serve."

Having seen and remembered, Willensky soon began exporting High Rock talent and ideas in what he called "reach-out" projects, going beyond the site itself into the larger community, expanding the center's capacity to serve. Among recent notable reach-outs was a special twenty-week community project involving participants (age eight to eighty) from a local "free school," an alternate high school, and a senior citizens center. The project investigated both the natural and man-made environments of Stapleton, an old Staten Island community that has been undergoing a variety of cultural and physical transitions. The work culminated in the marking of four "urban" trails though the community and clearly has fostered greater pride, self-awareness, and understanding among Stapleton residents. Technical services were supplied by High Rock through a grant from Museums Collaborative, Inc.

Another project, *Discover Staten Island*, featured bus tours to landmark houses and historic sites as well as to natural areas and such artificial features as the Fresh Kills Landfill. And there was *Worlds to Shape*—after-school workshops at the intermediate school level for students and teachers, exploring such diverse activities as mask-making, creation of sealed-world terrariums, and the design of sculptures animated by wind and sunlight. And *Mysteries of the Harbor*, a floating lecture series convened on the decks of ferryboats in transit, with a marine scientist holding forth on "how a striped bass holds its nose," a geologist on how the glaciers sculpted the harbor, a zoologist on the scavenging habits of seagulls, and a retired seaman on "recollections of an old sailor," among other salty topics.

In addition, Willensky fielded a number of workshops on environmental decision-making processes, using simulation games to involve civic leaders and social science teachers in the theories of community and environmental planning. He also commissioned Lois Gilman, a historian, to undertake a series of oral/video documentaries to be titled *Staten Island Remembered*. Funded by the New York State Council on the Arts, this project focuses on the island's agricultural, industrial, and recreational past, as remembered by local old-timers.

The other major new direction in which Willensky moved was toward a greater interaction with adults and families at the site itself. He was aware that walking a wood-chip footpath is not everyone's idea of how to spend a pleasant Sunday afternoon; that for many people who have never been to High Rock there must be a "better" reason than that to go there in the first place. So Willensky began to provide some reasons: free "forest fanfare" concerts (from woodwinds and trombones) under the trees at the council ring on Sunday afternoons in May;

The old "scout" shelter.

weekend workshops in nature photography, geology, natural gardening, crafts ("Primitive Pottery—from earth to fire without the tools of modern technology"), and even poetry . . . and all of these, in Willensky's words, "a wedding of art and nature though varied interpretations of the natural world." The result of such fanfare continued to surprise Willensky himself. "After some of the people who have come for the crafts or the concerts get here," he said, "they suddenly begin to recognize some of the natural symbols of the processes that control their lives. And they come back again and again—each time with a truly *better* reason to be at High Rock."

Of all the testimonials and tributes and assorted bits of advice left behind by High Rock's visitors in recent years, one, in particular, strikes me as a fitting coda to this piece. It turned up one day on a mimeographed questionnaire, where respondents are invited to put down what they feel High Rock should be considering in the way of *Do* and *Don't.* This respondent put pencil to paper and wrote:

> *"Don't get successful."*

A curious idea, all right—until you stop to think about it.

I do not mean to suggest here that true success is likely to spoil High Rock. True success, the way I figure it, is the achievement of quality—and *that* never spoiled anything. And, in that sense, High

Dragonfly.

Rock is getting more and more successful each passing year. So I think the respondent to the questionnaire must have had a different kind of success in mind. Like quantity. Like the triumph of numbers as a measure of achievement. Like counts and recounts of annual visitations, parking spaces, acres of institutional hard-top—each year, more and more. That is the kind of success that could kill High Rock, as misguided zeal and a bureaucratic bent for enumerated mass amusements at one time threatened to destroy the quality of America's finest national parks. But, as I mentioned before, I do not think that we will allow that sort of thing to happen. Not to High Rock, anyway. Given enough time, enough learned and joyous generations, it is conceivable that, someday, no one will have to think about saving High Rock from excess. Having built lovely receptivity into the human mind, High Rock at last will have saved itself.

Frog.

PART TWO

HIGH ROCK AND THE STATEN ISLAND GREENBELT TODAY (2011)

STATEN ISLAND GREEN
by Charles E. Little

Sitting on the rock at the far end of the loosestrife swamp, I find it easier to think about the past than the future. The future is such a far piece off. Of the future, you can be certain of only a very few things. The rock, for instance. It will be smaller tomorrow than it is today. You won't be able to measure that, but it's true. And the swamp, after many tomorrows, will be gone altogether, filled in with the bulk of its own natural decay. As for this butterfly of open space, this High Rock—who can say? It could be gone, too, stitched up in ragged seams. But only if we, in our individual lifetimes, allow it to happen. I do not think that we will.

—John G. Mitchell, *High Rock*

The first place I wanted to go on a recent visit to High Rock Park, a year after my friend John Mitchell "Mitch" had died, was that rock (see page 8). A glacial erratic, it had, for all I know, been brought down during the age of ice and planted, with its nearby loosestrife swamp, for the express purpose of being there for Mitch to write about and for Marbury Brown to draw in a way that could show both permanence and vulnerability.

What the rock asks, of course, is, Will this green sanctuary in all its fullness and diversity survive? Or will its essential meaning be ignored by a future generation, which with dynamite and a five-yard truck will move it out of the way so that more profitable uses of the land can be realized?

Mitch was, as usual, on the side of permanence. He had a generous view of the future, else why would he have invested so much in providing for it? And if this republication project proves anything, it is that the rock agrees and has every intention of prevailing. And, so, it is time not only to honor John Mitchell's work as author and conservationist, but also to add another chapter to the Staten Island Greenbelt story.

As Mitch relates, the Staten Island Greenbelt project got its start, as many do, with the threatened development of a valued tract, in this case seventy-two acres of secluded woodlands abutting the ridgeline of a low escarpment that rises at the center of Staten Island. In 1963, this acreage, called High Rock Camp, was put up for sale by the Girl Scouts of America to cash in on real estate prices that had inflated by 3,000 percent in the twelve years the Scouts had owned the land, due largely to the impact of the Verrazano Narrows Bridge, completed in 1964, which would open bucolic Staten Island to the kind of frenzied urban development going on everywhere in the New York City metropolitan region in those days. And, so, under the not-so-gentle prodding of Gretta Moulton, a Staten Island scout leader and conservationist, a campaign was mounted to induce the City of New York to buy the camp from a developer to whom it had been sold and to convert it into a conservation center.

But scarcely was the deal done than the High Rock land-savers realized that a highway project, the Richmond Parkway, a spur of the Staten Island Expressway, was planned to connect teeming Brooklyn with teeming New Jersey in such a way that its southbound lanes would run right along the edge of the new facility. Somehow the idea of a center meant to exemplify natural area conservation did not comport well with streaming traffic.

Adversity being the mother of invention, the High Rock advocates looked at the situation not only as a problem, but also as an opportunity. Do you suppose, they wondered, that we could stop the road from being built and use the right-of-way as a linchpin to preserve the entire ridge connecting a number of parks, preserves, and public open spaces? Well, why not?

Thus it was that a remarkable congeries of Staten Island conservationists began the process of turning a 4.7-mile-long, 300-foot-wide strip of woods, ponds, wetlands, and bouldery glades originally acquired by Robert Moses for a highway into an open-space corridor linking major public and quasi-public lands, such as the proposed site of the Staten Island Arboretum, Kaufmann Campgrounds, the William T. Pouch Boy Scout Camp, the Richmond County Country Club golf course, St. Francis Friary Woodlands, Deere Park, Reed's Basket Willow Swamp, Bloodroot Valley, La Tourette Park, and the new High Rock Park Conservation Center, which started it all.

At the same time, the as-yet-undeveloped path of the Willow-brook Parkway, which would have converged with Richmond Parkway, itself had become a de facto open-space corridor, linking the bay at Great Kills Beach (now part of the Gateway National Seashore) with the upland Greenbelt parcels. Withal, the effect of this proposed aggregation would be to nail down one of the largest greenspace areas in New York City. At 2,800 acres, it is four times the size of Central Park.

The problem was Robert Moses, America's greatest highway builder and a public works titan who characteristically brooked no interference. As a major public figure since the 1920s, he possessed more raw power than any other person in the city or state of New York, having created (in today's dollars) some $50 billion worth of highways and other public works in and around New York City. So when civic groups, led by the Staten Island Citizens' Planning Committee, brought suit for injunctive relief, Moses brushed them off, refusing to take the protest seriously and belittling the effort to save the ridge. He asserted archly that, without the civilizing influence of the road, the parklands would harbor all sorts of lurking cutpurses, arsonists, and hoodlums. John G. Mitchell, who had himself organized a protest group (SIGNAL— Staten Island Greenbelt-Natural Areas League, a masterpiece of acronymism), noted, "There are people [i.e., Moses] who actually cannot conceive of any valid form of outdoor recreation unless it is played out within earshot of moving pistons."

Robert Moses wouldn't budge. And yet, with protests, press releases, and citizen lawsuits, Mitchell and other civic leaders, many of them still active, fought the great parkway builder to a standstill. All in all, it took twenty years, from 1963 to 1983, for the Greenbelt to come into being.

As for High Rock, it was, and is, as Mitch wrote, the "buckle of the greenbelt" and, therefore, always in the middle of things. Thanks to the effort to save this natural area, an effort that had organized and inspired a broadly based civic leadership, the idea of a Staten Island Greenbelt had prevailed.

So it was that, by 1976, when *High Rock* was published, not only had a foundation been laid, but the basic concept had been fleshed out in important ways. Still, much has happened since then, including, notably, three major advances in terms of the management structure of the Greenbelt, the basic configuration and composition of the Greenbelt, and the open-space geography of the whole of Staten Island.

Regarding the first of these, after much delay the City of New York in 1984 recognized the existence of the Greenbelt as a unitary public facility rather than simply an unofficial aggregation of connected parks and private open spaces. And it was this action that effectively made the controversy over various highway alignments, as discussed in John Mitchell's *High Rock*, more or less moot (although not legally demapped). The proposal to provide official recognition was made by the New York City Planning Commission, whose 1983 study described the Greenbelt as "one of New York City's most beautiful and irreplaceable natural resources."

The key figure at this historic juncture was Thomas A. Paulo, New York City's parks commissioner for Staten Island. Paulo, a member of a prominent Staten Island family, earned a degree in environmental law as well as landscape architecture at Syracuse University, and he taught there for ten years. Then, during the early 1980s, seeing that Staten Island was headed for even more development trouble than in the 1960s, he returned home and got a job with the New York City Planning Commission. In preparing for the 1983 planning study, he walked, as he said, "every inch of the Greenbelt." However, the then-parks commissioner, Gordon Davis, would have none of the planning department's proposal to make the Greenbelt the responsibility of the Parks and Recreation Department. "The policy at that time was 'No new parks,'" Paulo told me. But then, by a great stroke of luck, Commissioner Davis was replaced by Henry Stern, who had pretty much the opposite view. And thus the Greenbelt, as of 1984, become the responsibility of the Parks and Recreation Department, as important, one might say, as Central Park, or Prospect Park, or any of the large units of the vast New York City parks system.

Having given the Greenbelt important governmental status and authority, Henry Stern then asked Mayor Edward I. Koch to create the position of "Greenbelt Administrator," which he did and which would be unlike any other park superintendency in the city. The area to be administered was not a real "park" but instead a collection of public, semi-public, and privately owned lands, each requiring different approaches in both property law and land management. And it would require, too, an ability to work with a large number of energetic constituencies and interest groups. Clearly, the man for the job was Tom Paulo, lawyer, landscape architect, planner, and well-known Staten Island figure.

A good deal of institutional imagination was needed to determine how to manage this large complex of green spaces that, while part of the Parks and Recreation Department, and having park ownerships within it, could not actually be managed as a park. The Staten Island Museum had been playing a role as a Greenbelt caretaker, but a new kind of management structure would be needed, Paulo realized, to make the Greenbelt an integral part of the civic life of Staten Island.

And so he decided to get a little help from his friends. Not from his fellow officials in the New York City government, mind you, but from the very people who had created this green-space mish-mash in the first place. So in 1987 he invited, to his home, the leaders of the Staten Island Citizens Planning Committee, SIGNAL, and the Greenbelt Emergency Conference—those who had so decisively preserved High Rock, dispatched the road builders, and brought the Greenbelt into being.

As Sally Williams, an early Greenbelt activist, describes it, "Tom brought all of us together and proposed the idea of a Staten Island Greenbelt Conservancy, to be a civic organization working directly with the parks department to manage and expand the Greenbelt. And so the Conservancy was formed, with just nine or ten of us. Tom is quiet about his accomplishments, but he did this on his own, on his own time."

The Greenbelt Conservancy was incorporated in 1989, "To foster education about the Greenbelt and its environs, promote public access and participation, and exercise prudent stewardship of the Greenbelt's lands, facilities, and endowment." Sally Williams was later to become a president of the Conservancy, a rotating office, held presently by Kathleen Vorwick. All those involved in the Conservancy praise Tom Paulo's accomplishment. Says Michael Dominowski, a former Conservancy official, "The lion's share of the credit for creating the Greenbelt management structure must go to Tom Paulo, for it was he who made it so."

The structure is not a simple one. The City of New York Parks and Recreation staff and Conservancy staff share offices in a remodeled residence in High Rock Park, and the Greenbelt's executive director is in charge of both. But what would sound like a structure bound to create tension between governmental agency responsibility and citizen-organization ideals has, by and large, worked out well. Certainly, this has been the case with Adena Long, who resigned in 2008 and was replaced by Robin A. Dublin. Fittingly, Long became the executive director of Vision Staten Island, a public-private organization charged with setting long-range planning goals for the borough, a focus on the future implied by the Greenbelt itself.

Another key date in the recent history of the Greenbelt is 1991, when, under the direction of Tom Paulo, the Conservancy and the Parks and Recreation Department collaborated on the Greenbelt master plan, with implementation funded by the city in 1993. The plan (now being updated) called for new acquisitions, such as Reed's Basket Willow Swamp; for new facilities, such as an environmental education center; for trail-making and signing; and for much else in a long to-do list that keeps getting done. As Tom Paulo modestly puts it, "If you stay around long enough, you finally get things resolved. You just hammer away."

As a result of its advocates keeping everlastingly at it, the Greenbelt today is a great green swath in the center of Staten Island with 2,800 acres of publicly owned parkland and private lands given protection as open space, plus a full complement of educational and recreational buildings and programs. Here are pristine natural areas with nearly forty miles of paths and trails; swamps, ponds, and wetlands; campgrounds and nature education programs; a $4 million nature center; a recreation center; two golf courses, one in public domain and the other protected by a ninety-nine-year lease; broad vistas across New York Harbor; intimate nooks and resting places; a "mountain" with an ironic name; a children's carousel and a demonstration garden; even a cemetery. All these features and more are recounted in Michael Twomey's *A Greenbelt Directory* (see pages 137–157).

In a cruel reprise of the great fight to save High Rock from being sold by the Girl Scouts in 1963, the Boy Scouts, nearly a half-century later, are now threatening to sell another key parcel of the Greenbelt for development. The 143-acre property, Pouch Camp, owned by the Boy Scouts of

America, is adjacent to High Rock and equally crucial to the integrity of the Greenbelt as a whole. The Scout's Greater New York Councils are hard-pressed to keep their day-camp program going on Staten Island but are waiting to see if some sort of solution to preserving the land will emerge. Land swaps have been proposed, as have open-space easements along with outright purchase with a combination of public and private funds. As Staten Island Borough President James P. Molinaro told environmental journalist Anne Schwartz, "We are researching every possibility of saving it in every possible way you can think of." Staten Island Congressman Michael E. McMahon is also on the case and has applied to the National Oceanic and Atmospheric Administration (NOAA) for a $3 million grant. With earlier grant requests, NOAA could provide as much as $6 million in all to save the camp.

Moreover, there is nothing like threat of losing a treasured part of the Greenbelt to stir the civic energies of Staten Island. Monster rallies, attracting thousands, have been staged in support of preserving Pouch Camp. Petitions have been circulated, producing tens of thousands of signatures. The Trust for Public Land, a heavy-hitting nonprofit land-acquisition organization, has been involved with the project. And the Staten Island Greenbelt Conservancy is in the thick of it. Says Kathy Vorwick, the Conservancy's President, "The concept of this 2,800-acre greenbelt, mostly in a natural state, would just be destroyed . . . if any portion of Pouch Camp were to be developed."

That is the bad news, at least at present. By contrast, the biggest piece of good news since John Mitchell's *High Rock* was first published is the creation of Fresh Kills Park, a 2,200-acre former landfill site now being converted to something absolutely spectacular. When completed, the park will connect in a more or less massive way the William T. Davis Wildlife Refuge with Southwest LaTourette to make a unitary green space of nearly eight square miles.

The Fresh Kills Landfill was established by the City of New York in 1949, and between then and March 2001, when the site was closed (although opened briefly after 9/11 to accommodate the search for the remains of the victims of the World Trade Center tragedy), some twenty garbage-filled barges, each carrying 650 tons, were shipped in every day to create, by the beginning of this century, four giant mounds, the tallest (at 225 feet) surmounting even the very tip of the Statue of Liberty's torch. And yet the landfill itself comprises less than half the site. The remainder (fifty-five percent) consists of ecologically rich wetlands, open waterways, and associated unfilled areas.

The conversion of the landfill into one of the park gems of New York City will be completed in 2037, according to plan. And the result will be not just a park, but an astonishing civil engineering achievement. On top of all that garbage—chicken carcasses, orange rinds, dead vermin, and a vast array of unspeakable urban fluids and solids—the city has deposited a thick layer of construction-site debris, of which there is God's plenty from the perpetual urban renewal project that is metropolitan New York. Then, covering the debris is an "impermeable membrane" of thick plastic. Throughout, pipes are laid to conduct methane gas, the by-product of decomposition, to the surface, and then over the pipes several feet of good clean soil are deposited, on top of which grass now grows and pathways will be constructed.

Actually, people will soon be able to enjoy some of the unique features of Fresh Kills, including its wetlands and its panoramic views of New York Harbor and the skyline of Manhattan. In time, thirty years from now, the decomposition process will be complete, the exhaust structures taken away, and most people who come to spend a happy day at Fresh Kills will be unaware of the redolent history of the site. By then, the full Monty in terms of park development will be available. *Architectural Record*, in an April 20, 2006 news item, summarized it this way: "The park will contain waterways for kayaking, an Olympic-level mountain biking course, and over 40 miles of trails and paths. Over 1,700 acres of the park will be devoted to undisturbed natural habitats. Programmed areas and commercial facilities such as boat marinas, banquet facilities, and an open-air market will be concentrated at the 'Confluence,' an area at the park's center where its three main creeks meet." And, as landscape architect and planner James Corner, of the University of Pennsylvania, told *New York* magazine, in its August 18, 2008 issue (herein slightly paraphrased), "The park is not only green and beautiful, it is a contemporary healing of the earth."

The green healing offered by making Fresh Kills a park was also much on the minds of participants at the Greenbelt forum, held at the College of Staten Island (the proceedings of which appear on pages 115–136). At this meeting of civic and governmental leaders, Eloise Hirsh, administrator of what will be known as Fresh Kills Park, was pummeled with questions about the current status of the park's development.

Large as it is, however, the proposed addition of Fresh Kills Park to the Greenbelt is not the only post-*High Rock* event. At Tom Paulo's office, the commissioner unfurled a map that covered most of a conference table, showing all the current and planned green spaces on Staten Island. The effect was a "Staten Island Green," a miracle of verdancy lying between the gray grittiness of Brooklyn and the industrial glut of New Jersey. As Paulo pointed out, the Greenbelt has itself helped engender additional green spaces (including the Fresh Kills Landfill) so that, in this borough of just under 500,000 people, there is more park and recreation acreage than in any other small city in the nation. "One-third of Staten Island is parks property," Paulo told me. "With Fresh Kills, we will have the biggest park system of any small city in the country."

This, then, is the third major post-*High Rock* bit of history or, better put, history-in-the making. That is to say, High Rock and the Greenbelt have become the land-use norm on Staten Island, not the exception, with the result that new parks and open spaces can be proposed without the kind of pro-development scorn heaped on those early tree huggers and daisy sniffers. Says Sally Williams, "The builders used to be our enemies, but now they see the Greenbelt as enhancing land values. Before, everybody was against us—Chamber of Commerce, political conservatives, highway people. Yes, there are individuals now who object sometimes but not organized groups."

Thus, it is not impossibly quixotic to propose connections trailways, bike paths, and linear parks—between the Greenbelt and open spaces along the eastern shore of the island fronting lower New York Harbor or along Arthur Kill, which separates Staten Island from New Jersey, or even to create major new destination parks for the linkages to connect with and then to create more linkages to make it all work together.

Along the south shore of Staten Island, where in the pre-Verrazano Narrows Bridge days the dairy farms were located, the Protectors of the Pine Oak Woods, an organization that took over where John Mitchell's SIGNAL left off, are pushing for a number of sites to be acquired by the Parks and Recreation Department, although not without some local resistance. Says Tom Paulo, "We've had amazing individuals—Ellen Pratt of the Protectors of the Pine Oak Woods, for—example who still take a lot of abuse for championing land preservation."

But the championing goes on apace, and Staten Island keeps getting greener and greener. So the question arises, "How did they do it?" Michael Dominowski answers it this way, in a letter he sent to me:

Well, you can't beat dumb luck. Or miracles, for that matter. There was probably nothing inevitable about the rescue of the great Frederick Law Olmsted's long-deferred dream of a chain of parks along the spine of Staten Island. What appears to have happened was a fortuitous confluence of circumstance and plain good fortune. New York had wearied of master-builder Robert Moses and his grasping, bullying ways. Staten Island was undergoing tumultuous change, thanks to that most Moses-like project the Verrazano Narrows Bridge, and that change, driven by money and deals done outside the public's eye, was coming on far too fast, and a cherished way of life was being laid waste.

Against this backdrop of change, Staten Island had the incredible good luck to have the likes of Gretta Moulton, John Mitchell, Bradford Greene, and all those many dedicated others enumerated in John Mitchell's book. They are civic heroes, every one.

All this is true, of course. But there is more to it.

Actually, these were a bunch of wild and crazy guys and gals. Young, or at least not old, and "full of chutzpah," as Sally Williams puts it. They went to every public meeting that could conceivably bear on the Greenbelt. They kept showing up at Robert Moses's office, asking for an appointment (read: showdown), which they never received, but their persistence must have driven Moses and his receptionist crazy. In *High Rock* (see *Part One*, pages 43–46), you can read about how Bob Hagenhofer embarrassed Nelson Rockefeller, the governor of New York, and how they got such a kick out of the fellow who accused them of being "*suede-o* conservationists."

Mary Lou Greene, wife of Brad Greene, the "father of the Greenbelt," says, "Well, it was fun! All these people enjoyed working together, being together. Bob Hagenhofer really was a very funny fellow. Terry Benbow was a bold, brash charge-ahead lawyer. Mitch was the wonderful writer and Brad the landscape architect who thought in visionary terms. And Sally Williams was a very League-of-Women-Voters-determined kind of lady.

"All had certain skills," said Mary Lou softly. "And they'd get together and drink a lot." Nothing like the unvarnished truth.

An important tactic in the long struggle was, and still is, the "ceremonial hike," a topic treated with at some length in *A Greenbelt Forum* (see pages 115–135). As has been mentioned, the key figure in establishing the Greenbelt in the early days was landscape architect Bradford Greene. Greene, who at this writing has just turned eighty-eight, had published a scholarly paper in 1961 pointing out that none other than Frederick Law Olmsted, creator (with Calvin Vaux) of Central Park, Prospect Park, and other seminal parks in New York City and across the nation, had long since proposed a trailway down the ridge that Moses had designated for his highway right-of-way.

So, taking a page from Supreme Court Justice William O. Douglas's earlier efforts to preserve the C & O Canal outside Washington, D.C., by staging highly publicized walks with famous public and political figures (actually Douglas stole the idea from John Muir), Mitchell, Greene, Hagenhofer, Williams, Benbow, and other members of the Greenbelt cadre organized hikes on "The Olmsted Trailway." With Senator Jacob Javitts, Secretary of the Interior Stewart Udall, and New York Mayor John V. Lindsay in tow along with many other political, civic, and conservation leaders, the Greenbelters let the land itself persuade the hikers of the importance of saving the ridge as open space.

The hikes were held in winter, for some perverse reason, but nevertheless hundreds of people would show up, strung out along the Olmsted Trailway for a half-mile or more. On one occasion in 1967 there had been a January thaw—common on Staten Island—and it had rained lightly, a misty rain, in the small hours of hike day, a Sunday. And then a sudden arctic front came through, freezing everything hard. By the time the hikers, including me, finally hit the trail at midmorning, the cold snap had not only sheathed the branches of trees and bushes with bright ice, but also created a jeweled arbor for the trail: tiny diamond droplets had frozen along the stems of catbriar and fox grape, transforming them into glinting garlands that lighted the way.

Perhaps that was the tipping point, when not even Robert Moses could stop the inexorable power of citizens who knew that the value of this place could not be measured in dollars or traffic counts but in nature's luminous vinestems strung across a woodland path.

And so the rock remains, a glacial erratic in more ways than one. And when you find it yourself on a walk through these woods and find perch on its flank to consider the importance of, say, loosestrife growing in a kettle pond, you are, in fact, sitting there with scores of others—Mitch, Bob, Gretta, and Terry among them. You can't see them, of course, but they are there. And they are glad to have your company.

A GREENBELT GALLERY
Photographs and Captions by Dorothy Reilly

The Gretta Moulton gate marks the entrance to High Rock Park, cornerstone of the Greenbelt. The gate was dedicated to the late Gretta Moulton in 1994, thirty years after she rallied citizens and elected officials to save High Rock from development. Bradford Greene, landscape architect and Gretta's friend, designed the gate, which received the prestigious Design Award from the New York City Art Commission. Many thousands of visitors pass through the Gretta Moulton gate each year seeking a quiet place to relax and learn about Staten Island's natural side.

Each year, as nature prepares for the winter months, visitors flock to High Rock for the great show of color. Long ago, native Indians utilized this land for sustenance and shelter; British soldiers camped here in 1776; early settlers explored its hills and valleys; and generations of Boy and Girl Scouts honed their outdoor skills on this venerable soil. Today, local naturalists hold the Greenbelt in high regard for its superb hiking.

Loosestrife Swamp, pictured here, is steps from the entrance to High Rock Park. A lovely earthen trail that transitions to a boardwalk along the swamp's edge wends its way around this wetland habitat. Spring peepers, tiny nocturnal amphibians not typically visible, inhabit the marshy swamp. Toward the end of March, the males emit a sleighbell-like chorus, signaling spring's arrival. On summer days, dragonflies dance across the swamp's surface as their wings reflect the sun's rays in this little slice of paradise.

For nearly two decades, the Greenbelt Conservancy has hosted a photography contest and exhibition that encourages New York City's students to interpret the Greenbelt through the camera's lens. The images submitted are as diverse as the students who submit them. Many photos have been published in Greenbelt journals and brochures. Students are asked to submit their photos along with a brief artist's statement, which inevitably results in eloquent and heartfelt essays and poems about the natural world and their place within it.

During the early 1960s, Robert Moses, the notorious New York City planner and Parks Commissioner, attempted to construct Richmond Parkway over Todt Hill, cutting through what is today's Greenbelt. Earth and rock blasted away for the highway was hauled to a remote area, eventually forming a 260-foot-high mound ironically nicknamed "Moses Mountain." The name stuck, but the parkway did not. Intrepid citizen-activists vigorously protested the highway and won their battle. Today, a steep hike up a much greener Moses Mountain rewards visitors with a panoramic view of the Greenbelt and New Jersey's Atlantic Highlands, fifteen miles in the distance.

Anticipation builds as one ascends the steep and rocky trail up Moses Mountain. There is only a small area at the "summit" for gazing and picture-taking, but most people agree: the view is worth the climb. For a densely populated area, it's refreshing to look as far as you can without seeing a single structure or road; only tree-tops are visible. Being above the tree line and closer to a bird's flight path than a car path shifts one's perspective in a profound way. The view is photogenic, and the resulting photo is proof that such a glorious spot of nature actually exists in New York City.

Scenes of nature abound in the Greenbelt. Sometimes they take your breath away. The dense woodlands pictured here stand in stark contrast to the hustle and bustle of the surrounding communities and to our increasing reliance on cell phones, email, and an all-embracing technological world. In the Greenbelt, one can relax and reflect, even chill out. A walk in the woods, where it is peaceful and quiet, is beneficial for the mind, body, and spirit. The Greenbelt is an oasis available to all.

With Staten Island's recent population boom came a loss of open space for recreation; thus, there was the need to designate certain areas for pedestrian use. The Greenbelt's newest trail—the 2.6-mile Multi-Use Trail—answers this call; it is a flat pathway that welcomes cyclists and walkers. A portion of it skirts the fairways of the La Tourette public golf course, a New York City landmark.

La Tourette Golf Course is an eighteen-hole public course that sets a high standard for public golf courses in New York City. Par is 72. The course sits on the grounds of the former David La Tourette farm (established in 1830). Two Revolutionary War battles took place within sight of the house, in the vicinity of nearby St. Andrew's Historic Church. The La Tourette family home, a stately Federal style brick structure built in 1836, has been converted to a clubhouse. The house was designated a New York City landmark in 1968 and in 1982 was listed in the U.S. Register of Historic Properties. Following a devastating fire in 2001, it was restored to its original splendor.

The 540-acre La Tourette Park, which encompasses the golf course, driving range, and surrounding trail system, is a highly active area within the Greenbelt, whatever the season. Several prestigious golf tournaments, including the Mayor's Cup, are held at La Tourette, winter snowfalls attract local children to La Tourette's rolling fairways for top-notch sledding, and the 2.6-mile-long Multi-Use Trail, which opened in 2009, is a boon for runners and cyclists year-round.

At 124 acres, the private Richmond County Country Club golf course, in the northeast section of the Greenbelt known as Todt Hill, offers undulating greens and distant views of lower New York Bay. In 1989, club members brokered a deal with New York State whereby the State purchased the land (as part of the 1986 Environmental Quality Bond Act) and, in turn, agreed to a ninety-nine-year lease agreement with the club. Revenues from the sale were set aside to establish an endowment fund for the Greenbelt Conservancy.

Willowbrook Park, one of the Greenbelt's most popular destinations, is a perfect staging area for large-scale Greenbelt events, such as the annual Pumpkin Festival. Year-round, the 164-acre park offers ball and archery fields, a playground, picnic grove, pond-side relaxation, catch-and-release fishing, as well as the magnificent Carousel for All Children.

96

Opened in 1999 and maintained by the Greenbelt Conservancy, the charming and aptly named Carousel for All Children is reminiscent of a by-gone era. The Victorian-inspired attraction consists of fifty-one hand-carved and painted figures of traditional wooden horses, mythical beasts, and endangered species. Forty original renderings of Staten Island landmarks embellish the carousel's housing and provide a history lesson for parents while their children take a spin, unless the parents are taking a ride, too!

The Greenbelt Nature Center is a hub for activities and programs. Visitors can obtain a map and access the Greenbelt's trail system, sign up for programs and activities, speak with a Greenbelt representative, or just relax and enjoy the beautiful wooded grounds. The 5,000-square-foot stone and wood structure has a low, earth-hugging design that blends with its natural surroundings. The interior contains the Richmond County Savings Foundation exhibitions, which explain the Greenbelt's history and ecology.

High Rock Park was designated a National Environmental Education Landmark by the U.S. Department of the Interior in 1971. School and enrichment programs serve students from pre-school to college-level, instilling early in life a heartfelt appreciation for the natural world and a real sense of what it takes to maintain it.

Greenbelt Summer Camp is a longstanding tradition for local children. On any given day, happy campers might encounter turtles and frogs and other critters in their natural habitat, explore rugged trails, learn to use a hula hoop or read a compass, or simply contemplate the history and existence of this undeveloped section of Staten Island. In the not-too-distant future, these young citizens will become caretakers of the Greenbelt; the experience and knowledge gathered during carefree summer days will prepare them to be responsible naturalists and stewards of the Greenbelt.

The Greenbelt's hiking trails, nearly forty miles of them, are maintained and improved by a natural resource management team comprised of staff members, volunteers, and student interns. The Greenbelt encourages people of all ages to join its volunteer corps and play an active role in the stewardship of the park.

*Located off the Blue/Yellow Trail in High Rock Park, Pump House Pond is
an example of a kettle pond formed by melting chunks of receding glacier. It is
perfectly situated for Greenbelt educators to conduct "pond dips" with eager young
naturalists. Students analyze water samples and research plant and animal life,
including turtles, frogs, and water snakes.*

Willowbrook Lake in the 164-acre park of the same name is a perfect spot to cast a line for catch-and-release fishing in the Greenbelt. Constructed in 1932, Willowbrook Lake was the first human-made pond on Staten Island. The park's central location makes it easily accessible, yet it is isolated enough from the hustle and bustle of the surrounding area. Willowbrook Park is one of the Greenbelt's most-visited areas; it boasts baseball and archery fields, tennis courts, a shaded picnic grove, playground, the Carousel for All Children, hiking trails, and more. The park is adjacent to the 240-acre College of Staten Island campus, a branch of the City University of New York.

Walker Pond, in the southeastern corner of High Rock Park, is named after the Walker family, whose house and barn overlooked the pond until it was demolished in the 1960s. The five Walker children grew up in a woodland setting, with just a lighthouse and one other homestead as distant neighbors. Today, the neighborhood of New Dorp Heights, with hundreds of single-family dwellings, surrounds Walker Pond. A small dock, which was dedicated in 2008 to the late Tommy Monahan, a young boy who loved nature, allows visitors to observe the turtles, lily pads, dragonflies, and birds that make their home in this special place.

There are moments of discovery in childrens' lives when something new and fasci-
nating captivates their minds and imaginations. In the Greenbelt, one can witness
such a revelation on any given day. Whether it's a handsome turtle, the tickle
of a caterpillar on a small hand, the rustling of a chipmunk, a hawk dipping
overhead, or a migration of monarch butterflies, eyes and smiles widen as a child's
curiosity is piqued. Learning can begin and never end in the Greenbelt.

Whether alone or in a group, the Red-spotted purple butterfly is a delight to behold for young and old.

*This example of Queen Anne's Lace (*Daucus carota*), or wild carrot, was found along the Yellow Trail on the way to Moses Mountain. A native to temperate regions of Europe, Queen Anne's Lace prefers a disturbed area which it helps to re-naturalize. While not an indigenous species, it is nonetheless delicate, beautiful, and photogenic and is treasured along with native species that balance the ecosystem.*

The Greenbelt summer camp experience affords "young naturalists" opportunities to paddle, hike, explore, and observe—all in nature's backyard. One recent summer day, with the assistance of Greenbelt environmental educators and New York City Urban Park Rangers, campers learned to navigate a canoe while experiencing the pleasures that go with it. For many children, this is their first experience paddling. Children who visit the Greenbelt often, however, whether on the water or the trails, gain a fresh perspective of the natural world. These experience shape their lives and will influence their future philosophies.

A GREENBELT FORUM
Moderated by Deborah Popper

As an integral part of this republication project, some twenty-three organizational and governmental officials, academics, and citizen conservationists gathered on September 20, 2008, in a conference room at the College of Staten Island (CSI), City University of New York, to discuss a little bit of the past and a great deal of the future of the Staten Island Greenbelt. What follows is an edited transcript (by Charles E. Little) of that meeting. The participants are the following:

Alan Benimoff, Professor of Geology, College of Staten Island

David Burg, President, Wild Metro

Maritza Cuevas, Director of Education, Staten Island Greenbelt, New York City Department of Parks and Recreation

Michael Dominowski, Assistant Managing Editor, Staten Island Advance, and a former board member of the Greenbelt Conservancy

Richard Flanagan, Professor of Political Science, College of Staten Island, and Director of the Staten Island Project at CSI

Bradford Greene, landscape architect and founder of the Staten Island Citizens Planning Committee

Steven Handel, Director of the Center for Urban Restoration Ecology, Rutgers University

Eloise Hirsh, Administrator, Fresh Kills Park, New York City Department of Parks and Recreation

James Kaser, Archivist, College of Staten Island

Charles E. Little, author and editor

Adena Long, Executive Director, Vision for Staten Island

Alison C. Mitchell, conservationist

Judy Nachison, conservationist

Thomas Paulo, Borough Commissioner for Staten Island, New York City Department of Parks and Recreation

Deborah Popper, Professor of Political Science, Economics, and Philosophy, College of Staten Island, City University of New York, and Visiting Professor, Princeton University's Environmental Institute

Frank Popper, Professor of Urban and Regional Planning, Rutgers University

Ellen Pratt, Board of Directors, Protectors of the Pine Oak Woods

Tony Rho, Greenbelt Natural Resources Manager, New York City Department of Parks and Recreation

Henry Stern, former Commissioner, New York City Department of Parks and Recreation

Kathleen Vorwick, Greenbelt Conservancy Board President

Sally Williams, former Board President, Greenbelt Conservancy

After a welcome by Dr. Tomás D. Morales, President of the College of Staten Island, the discussion began.

Why We Are Here

DEBORAH POPPER: Thank you all for coming. We are here to think about the future of the Staten Island Greenbelt, as part of the republication of the late John G. Mitchell's wonderful book, *High Rock: A Natural and Unnatural History*. The republication project is being led by Alison C. Mitchell, who is with us today, as is the project editor, Charles E. Little. I suppose some might ask, Why republish a book about a fight that was won thirty years ago? Well, I think there are lots of reasons to do so. To begin with, High Rock and the Staten Island Greenbelt have changed. What began as seventy-six acres became 2,800 acres and will soon be almost doubled with the addition of

Fresh Kills Park. So, it is all sort of done, isn't it? And all secure? Well, maybe not. And that's where this forum comes in—a re-examination of High Rock, the Greenbelt, Fresh Kills, and where Staten Island is going: that is what we'll talk about this morning. I've asked Tom Paulo to start us off.

THOMAS PAULO: Deborah insisted that we were not to approach the book backwards, which means that from today forward is where we're going, and that is good. Although there are some here who were the originators of the Greenbelt idea, there are others in careers associated with the Greenbelt whose jobs didn't exist when a small group of citizens set about to save High Rock and make a Greenbelt. In fact, open space preservation is today much more of a governmental responsibility than it was for those citizens. And subsumed under the term "open space" are natural areas, athletic fields, historic sites, even the now-closed Fresh Kills landfill—so many different places that concerned only the "kooks" in the 1960s. And, I guess for those of us who were around in those days, that's what we were: kooks. A bunch of nuts. Robert Moses called us "the daisy sniffers."

But now all of that has been put aside. College departments teach about open space, scholars research it. And governments have, indeed, discovered the environment. So, as bad as things may seem, they're a lot better than they were forty years ago. We've got a Greenbelt. But, in making the Greenbelt "official," we soon realized that city planning doesn't operate it in terms of generalized open spaces. So we had to find a way to make our Greenbelt become a physical reality as well as something that was cared for. At the time there was a Parks Commissioner by the name of Gordon Davis, and, when I presented the Greenbelt planning study, he said, "Parks is not going to take this over. Just want to make it clear." So now we had to hammer up some kind of rather ridiculous management scheme. But guess what happened? Three months later, Henry Stern became the Parks Commissioner, and that changed the whole involvement of the Parks and Recreation Department, not only in this instance, but in so many areas where you wouldn't have had stewardship in the government taking care of something. Henry was one of the leaders who moved the department from simply being associated with traditional parklands into the area of preserving open spaces and, in particular, significant natural areas.

So the effort crept along over time, but with amazing results in the end. Now we've got Fresh Kills and the daunting task of converting these 2,200 acres into a park, with a lot of citizen encouragement.

And that is the point. On Staten Island, it's the *people* who have learned how to preserve open space. The original groups, among them the Staten Island Citizens Planning Committee, John Mitchell's SIGNAL [Staten Island Greenbelt-Natural Areas League], Protectors of the Pine Oak Woods, and others—have fashioned a process involving citizen groups and government agencies to make things happen. And so, today, one-third of Staten Island is open space, including park land. No community of our size in the country, I think in the world, has that large a percentage of open space. Forty years ago something started. And it is still going on.

D. POPPER: With that, please, everybody feel free to jump in. There are a lot of issues here. For example, to what extent does the Greenbelt influence what's *not* open space? And to what extent do we need to make sure that there are corridors connecting disparate open space areas?

A Matter of Habitat

STEVEN HANDEL: Well, I'd like to comment on that. I'm a plant ecologist, and my basic academic interest is in how plants reproduce and spread and what determines how plants support the critters that live in an area. Urban areas are very interesting because they're so drastically altered—the kinds of plants and animals that live here change rapidly. We have new species coming in from Europe and Asia which challenge our historic biodiversity. The only way to stop the degradation is to make links to allow natural corridors for our heritage of indigenous species to persist.

You have a lot of green spaces in Staten Island and a lot more being planned, most notably Fresh Kills with more than 2,000 acres. Tom Paulo said that one-third of Staten Island is open space. Well, the other two-thirds, where we live, can also play a role. I don't see any particular reason why the suburban parts of Staten Island can't support the preserved natural areas with native plantings and careful management of backyards and frontyards, so the borough as a whole can be more sustainable. If you just have pieces of green here and there, they are all at risk, ecologically. By connecting spaces, and adding bits and pieces, we can save the protected land.

HENRY STERN: Can I ask a question? All this talk about the invasive plants and species sounds like you're anti-immigration. Are all exotic species bad? [Laughter.]

HANDEL: Almost all new species are bad. Staten Island has lost about forty percent of its natural heritage—plants that have been eliminated by infrastructure development as well as through competition from invasive plants from other continents. It's not the rare orchids someone brings in, it's the aggressive weeds. Those are the ones really damaging our parks and open spaces. This city is spending millions now on trying to kill the climbing bittersweet vine, among other problem species, which are taking over what were the original native-plant habitats.

STERN: Do you work on the Asian longhorned beetle?

HANDEL: That's gotten a huge amount of attention, and a lot of money is being spent to try to stop it from killing all our shade trees.

TONY RHO: I'm a natural resource manager, and managing invasive species is a big component in my job. There's always a lack of funds because invasive plants and animals really move a lot quicker than municipalities can keep up with. It's a difficult challenge.

D. POPPER: How do such resource management issues native species, exotics—fit into what is happening at Fresh Kills, which is a totally disturbed landscape, not a natural area?

ELOISE HIRSH: Actually, native species plant management has everything to do with how we are planning the park. In fact, our first project within the boundary of the landfill will be a seed farm, where we will be propagating "founder seed" plants for native species production.

PAULO: I would like to make a comment about the actual corridors that Steve mentioned. As open space segments fall into place, we do look at the connection points. It's ironic that the deer population has shown us where the linkages are, from the New Jersey shore all the way up into the Greenbelt and along the Richmond Creek system.

D. POPPER: What are the obstacles to pulling it together? Outside the Greenbelt.

PAULO: Roads are the primary problem. But, even there, using the Richmond Creek as an example, the deer go under Richmond Avenue through a culvert that crosses the road. So, where there is that large an opening, linkage is possible. This suggests that where you have drainage areas, either make sure there are no roads that interrupt a linkage or make sure that there is enough open space created so creatures can move though.

ELLEN PRATT: There's another area where a conglomeration of open spaces provides for linkages and species interchange on the South Shore of Staten Island. This includes Mt. Loretto, both the ocean side and the inland side, and Lone Pond Park, which is yet to be dedicated, and Millcreek, Bluebelt, and the Butler Woods, which is down on the shorefront. The whole area totals about 425 acres, which is relatively contiguous and large enough in size to succeed in terms of wildlife.

PAULO: Ellen makes a good point. Size is a big factor in terms of habitat—the bigger the land area is, the more likely it is that species will be able to survive. It's when you get these little fragmented areas that Dr. Handel was talking about that you don't have a success rate.

KATHLEEN VORWICK: With regard to protecting large habitat areas, one of the things the Greenbelt Conservancy has been working on for the last year or so is to look at the master plan, completed in the early 1990s, and strategize on how to make a larger Greenbelt, no matter what the ownership might be—whether it's parks, private land, or Fresh Kills. In the course of this work, we emphasize that every component should be part of the whole picture in terms of habitat and not subject to fragmentation. People taking a couple of acres here and a couple of acres there, whether it's for roads or for some other project, has been an ongoing threat. We need to understand that larger is better and that corridors are important.

FRANK POPPER: Does the city have long-term funding for habitat restoration? And are acquisitions included in your master plan?

VORWICK: It's more of a guideline, with specifics such as the million-tree initiative. Tony Rho has led the effort in planting 2,000-plus trees in areas that are not already forested within the Greenbelt. And there are a couple of brownfield sites that we're looking at for remediation which are part of the Greenbelt.

Roads and Recreation

F. POPPER: Is there a policy to acquire more shoreland property to provide greater connectivity? Would that be part of any possible expansion of the Greenbelt?

VORWICK: Within the Greenbelt itself, we have the Amundsen Trailway, which was originally mapped as the Willowbrook Parkway, now abandoned, although still on the official map. So a trailway—the White Trail—now runs from High Rock Park down to the seashore, and it is used by joggers, bicyclists, and hikers. So, in this way we connect shoreline habitat to upland habitat via this recreational corridor.

F. POPPER: Is shorefront parkland likely to expand in the future?

VORWICK: Well, hopefully it will, if we ever get this highway issue settled once and for all. In the meantime, we're using the trailway as if a mapped right-of-way were not there.

STERN: The environmental community has been trying for years to de-map the highway, and it has not been successful. Bills have been introduced to do it in both the Senate and the Assembly, but they have been blocked. I suspect the city is behind this because it wants to reserve its options for the future, and it knows it'll never get it mapped again.

One unique problem in Staten Island is that the elected officials who boast about the parks in their campaign material, videos, and so on have done their best to oppose open space acquisitions and to prevent the growth of parks and to put roads through. I remember when I was Commissioner, fighting with Borough President Molinari, trying to save trees. We lost two trees in the zoo which didn't have to be removed but were taken down almost out of malice. That's the problem we face here. It's not the majority of the residents, it's the officials. Of course, Tom can't say anything about this kind of thing. [Laughter.]

PAULO: Oh, I've said a lot about it. In fact, I do think there is a disconnect as the commissioner has pointed out. With regard to road building, kids today are probably thinking far less about driving an SUV. And they are not doing team sports. They are not doing what we were doing. In survey research the college did on transportation, young people said they wanted more public transportation, not roads. That's the disconnect. The younger generation is far more aware of what is important than the current elected officials are.

D. POPPER: Well, what would that mean specifically in terms of recreation for younger people the recreation that's being planned for in parks?

PAULO: We call them the "X-sports," the self-challenging activities. Part of problem is today's schedules; you can't always get a lot of people together. So, if you want exercise, you do it on your own whether it's the biking or jogging or whatever. That's the direction.

The Uses of Fresh Kills

HIRSH: When you're planning for recreation on 2,200 acres, as we are at Fresh Kills, and talking to a lot of people, you end up with a menu of everything for everybody. So there are playing fields and hiking trails and mountain biking trails and pedestrian and equestrian trails and so on. But, in the end, the landscape determines what we can actually have in terms of facilities. That's the big point that we are trying to get across to the public. This is a former landfill. It is a completely engineered landscape, and for the next thirty years the landfill infrastructure will determine what we can build and where we can build it.

I'm sure many of you are familiar with the master plan, but what I'd like to tell you about is that we actually are beginning to build some projects on the periphery. One is the Owl Hollow soccer fields in the southern portion and the other a small neighborhood park—Schmul Park—in the Travis section. This is an incredibly exciting little park with lots of color in it, and it will provide an entrance to Fresh Kills Park itself.

It's difficult to speak in public about Fresh Kills because, aside from the places on the edges, nothing's there yet, and it's hard for people to believe that actually anything ever will, in fact, happen. So, that's why we elected to do two projects within the confines of Fresh Kills that the New York State Department of Environmental Conservation couldn't say anything about. So we can actually start building them. The first is a native-plant seed farm with a wonderful path that will let people get from a parking lot out to the water. We've always thought that the first projects we do, even if they turn out to be small in acreage, should get people to the water and to let people get on top of one of the mounds. The water and a view of the expanse of landscape really defines what Fresh Kills is all about.

This is the good news, but, again, people mustn't forget that we'll be sharing the site with the Department of Sanitation for the next thirty years at least. The landfill infrastructure is what defines what we'll be able to do with the park.

STERN: Eloise, maybe you should say just what the infrastructure is, what's left over from the landfill.

HIRSH: It's not left over. It's still active. One system manages the methane gas, and it's a design challenge to have a park with gas-well pipes sticking up on every acre. Working with our fabulous geotechnical engineering team and with terrific cooperation from the Sanitation Department, we are making sure not only that the landfill infrastructure is safe, but that the public is safe. We have figured out a way to make something like manholes that are at grade, and we'll put at least two feet of new soil everywhere.

HANDEL: These needs for methane collection will fade over time. Obviously, we need a long view, for this is a spectacular site. I've had the honor of being on top of those mounds, and it's a spectacular park. Eventually, the garbage will decompose, and then Fresh Kills will simply be a public amenity in the traditional sense.

You know, we talk about plant species and natural features in a traditional environmental idiom. But we should also see these features in terms of "ecosystem services"—how the park areas can serve people in terms of public health. This has tremendous traction politically in justifying high-cost parks and open spaces. I always say we want to build a park not just for the wild flowers and the migratory birds, but because it provides clean, cool air, clean ground water, mental health, urban aesthetics, culture. And people, particularly people in government, listen to this kind of argument because it makes sense and, it saves money.

PAULO: When you say saving money, let me ask Eloise to go into greater detail on the soil requirements at Fresh Kills.

HIRSH: That's one reason why this project won't be saving anybody any money for a long time. The Department of Environmental Conservation [DEC] has "brownfield" regulations on how clean the soil has to be in order for the public to step on it. If it's commercial use, it's one thing. If you're going to have houses on it, it's another, and active recreation is yet another. Actually, the level of allowable contaminants for recreation are in the middle. Residential standards require the highest level of cleanliness since people may be planting tomatoes on it, and the kids are eating them.

But landfills are covered by a quite different set of regulations, and the DEC is saying that, rather than the middle-level recreation-grade soil (which probably is cleaner than that of any other park in the city), we will be held to the residential standard. That means that the fill at Fresh Kills is going to be really expensive and will have to come from pristine areas. Unfortunately, the high cost will limit how much acreage we can actually have open for the public.

HANDEL: Dirt isn't cheap.

PAULO: It's an interesting situation where you have an environmental regulatory agency setting a standard that may potentially reduce the size of a site meant to improve the environment.

NIMBYs and the Banana People

D. POPPER: Actually, that's one of the questions I wanted to talk a little bit more about—how the different government agencies work together. Eloise, you said that you have a wonderful relationship with the sanitation department.

HIRSH: That's right.

D. POPPER: And we've been talking about the DEC. Are there any lessons from the good relationships or the bad relationships?

STERN: Well, in my experience, it's rarely a matter of sweet-talking people. Eloise is a professional, and she's not rude to anybody. Dumb as they might be. [Laughter.]

PAULO: That's right.

STERN: What happens is that some people are institutionally opposed to progress. Either they just want roads, or they don't want public money spent on recreation or poor people in the neighborhood—that's what's blocked the development of Gateway National Seashore for the last twenty-five years. The national parks are usually funded for capital construction by the local congressperson. It's an earmark. But, in the Gateway, the neighbors didn't want the park because they felt it would draw minorities and others to a previously all-white neighborhood. So that's opposition on the right. There's also opposition on the left from the purists who don't want you to touch anything. The NIMBY people, "not in my backyard," have been succeeded by the banana people. And, the banana people say, "Build absolutely nothing, anywhere, near anybody."

The New York State DEC is the worst in this regard because the kind of people who work there, who decide to make their careers in conservation, believe that everything should be preserved, and whatever interferes with that should not be allowed like those soil issues. They're advocates for one point of view. And it's very difficult to deal with. It's not personal. It's institutional.

HIRSH: Well, you have to accept what the site has been for the last fifty years, if you're going to go forward into the next fifty. And that means accepting and understanding what the regulations are and understanding the obligations of other departments and what their kind of stewardship means. Actually, there are a lot of guys on the site who are genuinely excited about the possibilities for this place as a natural area, who have been giving Audubon tours for years. There are guys on the site who know as much about nature and wildlife as anybody in this room. There is a genuine feeling for the potential of the site among a lot of the people who've been working on it. My husband actually was Sanitation Commissioner in the Lindsey administration. And even then there were people who were interested in the future of Fresh Kills.

The Politics of Citizen Participation

D. POPPER: I'd like to invite David Burg to jump into this conversation—whenever you'd like . . .

DAVID BURG: I'm the president of a group called Wild Metro. I have a personal background both as a professional naturalist and in real estate, which is an interesting combination for an environmentalist. At Metro, we found a strong need for an organization whose focus is protecting nature where people live. There are groups to save the whales and groups to save the Amazon and to save the wilderness and to save the wolves. But, in an urbanizing world, unless you save nature where people live, you have diminished the human experience. I am not worried about the bananas. I'm not worried about the people who are trying to save something because, the truth is, it's a tiny minority with almost no power and only rarely wins a battle.

The larger issue on Staten Island that Wild Metro has been trying to understand is how people here become inspired to preserve green space resources such as the Greenbelt.

D. POPPER: Yes, how do you build a constituency for that kind of preservation?

SALLY WILLIAMS: Well, certainly a number of persons around the table can talk about that. Alison and Judy know about the early days and our walks through the proposed route of the Richmond Parkway, helping people understand what building the highway would destroy and giving them a vested interest in the landscape.

D. POPPER: How did you get them out? How did you get their participation?

WILLIAMS: We bribed them. [Laughter.]

D. POPPER: You bribed them?

WILLIAMS: We offered free pea soup, sherry, apples . . .

JUDY NACHISON: And an afternoon in the woods . . .

ALISON MITCHELL: And a family outing.

HIRSH: We're also engaged in citizen participation. I'm sure many of you have been on our Fresh Kill tours.

STERN: Is there a Friends of Fresh Kills group?

HIRSH: Not yet, but I'm sure there will be.

VORWICK: I don't mean to get off topic, but what strikes me is how hard it is to accept each other's reality on Fresh Kills as well as other places. Sometimes, when we meet with elected officials, we know instinctively that they have a totally different mindset than we might wish. Do you think there would be anything to be gained by scheduling meetings between us, the Greenbelt Conservancy, and other groups, with the borough president and his engineering staff? Ask them how they conceive some of their reality. Rather than us against them.

HIRSH: Actually, a lot of progress has been made with the borough president's recent offering of compromise on where the roads might be. And on the wind energy issue.

WILLIAMS: The most important thing is to get elected officials to understand the realities. Eloise and her team have certainly made the effort to go out and talk to civic groups. Now, civic groups have taken on an expanded role in the last thirty years in Staten Island. They've become more vocal all around the island. I think a good way to get people involved is in a one-on-one situation, where they can ask questions, which you can't do effectively at large forums.

HIRSH: Creating the Greenbelt offers a wonderful lesson in that.

STERN: In my experience, the political culture of Staten Island is very different from the other four boroughs. On Staten Island, the activists are more conservative, sort of Sarah Palin types, with the other boroughs having more radical activists. For example, I think Adrian Benepe is a very good commissioner of the Parks [and Recreation] Department, but it's been sued loads of times. For every project in Manhattan, there are objections. The point is, there's a culture that opposes things that any government agency puts forward. And you have to deal with that. But the Greenbelt is a triumph. And I'm sure Eloise will do the same with Fresh Kills. You have to tread very carefully in these things. Rule 28N. The natives are restless tonight. [Laughter.]

D. POPPER: But how has the civic culture changed in Staten Island in the last, what, thirty to forty years since the work on the Greenbelt started? Is some different approach needed now? Are there different ways of working with the civic groups?

PRATT: Now we have community boards, and they take away a lot of the excitement and energy of the civic groups. Members of these groups tend to be co-opted by the community boards, which supposedly represent the interest of the public. I say, quote, "supposedly."

STERN: The point is, the community boards are appointed by the borough president.

PAULO: So it's totally politicized.

VORWICK: I'll give you a for-instance of just how politicized. I attended a community board hearing, and a certain politician's videographer was there taping the proceedings concerning Fresh Kills. Every member of that community board he had appointed was being videotaped as to the questions they asked and the responses they made. So, there's just no validity to any community board decision. Adena may disagree because she's on the Community Board, but . . .

ADENA LONG: Yes, but I recused myself from that meeting precisely because of that sort of thing.

D. POPPER: Do you see a way to form an alternative structure for citizen participation? A way toward more authentic civic action? Doesn't your Greenbelt Conservancy sort of see itself as part of some kind of reform effort?

VORWICK: We have to be nice to everyone. For instance, Adena was successful in getting two hybrid vehicles for our environmental education program because something like that is not controversial. There's no battle there. But on the highway demapping issues, which affect us decisively, that's another situation. Even though it was approved by the assembly committees, the demapping legislation was not successful because the discussion was all behind the scenes, and we had no firsthand knowledge of it.

HIRSH: The question is, What's needed for the civic culture to be effective? And, in this regard, the role that academic institutions can play is crucial, particularly in Staten Island because of the community boards and what has happened because of them. If academic institutions can have a public role, they can generate the civic dialogue and give some heft to organizations that might not otherwise have it.

HANDEL: I agree that academic institutions can play a useful role. I'm very aware, as you are, of the distrust of public officials by many of our citizen groups. Once we had a meeting about Fresh Kills that Deborah chaired some years ago, and the commissioner of public health of New York City stood up and said, "We've done air testing, and the air around Fresh Kills is just fine." Nobody believed him. But, now, I'm impressed that the current mayor [Bloomberg] has this Green New York idea to plant a million trees, add 2,000 acres of habitat, and so forth. The pendulum has really swung, and I would think that, here in Staten Island and especially with academic involvement, you could grab onto that pendulum for a lot of environmental initiatives.

F. POPPER: I think it's important to point out how different our world is from the world forty years ago, when work on the Greenbelt started. Universities weren't prominent as players in these sorts of things. What they could bring to the table barely existed in terms of environmental sciences compared to today. The environmental impact statement process itself did not exist at that time. But now we are all thinking more environmentally in a way that legitimizes those pioneering kooks who got involved with this stuff in 1965. One sees this not just in Staten Island but a zillion different environmental controversies around the world.

Environmental Education and the Greenbelt

MARITZA CUEVAS: Well, you all have brought a lot of topics to the table, but I think one underlying theme that engages everyone here is raising awareness. In this regard, what I'm taken with is my experience with the children who come to the Greenbelt. We get children who have never been in a forest reserve, and the impact of a field trip, a field trip to the Greenbelt, is incredible. These are children of diverse background, but they are all so taken with this kind of natural environment, they can hardly wait to return. And they influence their parents when they go back home and talk about their field trip.

So, raising environmental awareness in our community and beyond is the key. In this regard, we are in partnership with the College of Staten Island. We have a group coming up this week for the environmental ethics class. College kids hiking High Rock. So we have a chance to raise their awareness of the issues that are present in High

Rock. Our role is to educate, to raise awareness—not to advocate. To present the facts and the issues.

D. POPPER: In connection with environmental education, are there particular things that you would like this college to do?

ALAN BENIMOFF: Yes, we have the Center for Environmental Science here that can do this kind of work.

CUEVAS: You teach it here, but the general public is not environmentally aware of what's going on. They're so overwhelmed with the day-to-day responsibility of being parents and working and commuting. That's our role at the Greenbelt, at the nature center to present programs to the general public to make them aware.

MICHAEL DOMINOWSKI: I think the Greenbelt's education program is absolutely on the right track. It comes down to a pretty basic thing as far as I can see—people will preserve the things that they love, they love the things that they know, and they know the things that they are taught. So, if we can teach them to be comfortable with nature, to be engaged in it, to appreciate it, we can succeed.

RHO: A big chunk of what I do is try to put the environmental science research generated at CSI into action on a lot of different projects that focus on restoration. We work with volunteers, ranging from children to adults, and we teach them about problems for ecosystems—soil erosion, invasive plants. And we try to put the research into action, to correct some of these problems. I'm also working on a massive vegetative community assessment and mapping project for the entire 2,800 acres, using a specific methodology that was developed with the college. Once we assess everything we've identified, we'll draft a specific plan, and we are looking forward to partnering with other institutions on implementation.

Smart Growth for Staten Island

RICHARD FLANAGAN: Expanding on the educational mission a bit, the opinion polling we've done at the college shows that the driving, thumping issue on Staten Island is just getting around—transportation—and trying to solve our basic transportation problems. Public opinion is the whip, and elected officials are beginning to feel it. In the congressional campaign now, the candidates are talking about going to Washington and bringing back earmarks for mass transit. This is called "smart growth," but that cuts two ways, doesn't it? A better mass transportation system is going to affect open spaces because the flip side of that is that, in metropolitan core areas like Manhattan, land prices will go up, and consequently there will be more pressure to turn more of the land out here in Staten Island into homes so people can quickly get to Manhattan.

New York City's relationship to a smart-growth philosophy is a strange one. It had smart growth before smart growth became a trend in other parts of the country or even next door in New Jersey. New York City did smart growth 100-150 years ago with the placement of its mass transit systems, and then more or less forgot about it. But Staten Island needs the kind of approach that we see in other parts of the country. In New York City, it's built in, so our bureaucracy isn't giving us what the borough of Staten Island may need.

This spring the college hosted a forum on housing, and I ended up spending a lot of time talking to developers on Staten Island. The one theme I heard was, "Well, you know, we have all these little brownfield spots, and I can't afford to fill those in. But, if you want to talk about a big transit village on the West Shore, a multi-billion dollar project, well, that's exciting stuff." But then, how much open space would such a project eat up? So, it seems to me there has to be a public opinion shift to have Staten Islanders think effectively about smart growth.

STERN: But what exactly is "smart growth"? Sounds like plant food. [Laughter.]

FLANAGAN: Well, an important aspect of it is to have concentrations of housing around mass-transit centers that will decrease dependence on cars and allow you to use your land more efficiently.

F. POPPER: As Rich points out, in New York we had a smart growth before smart growth was cool. In many ways, New York appears to be one of the most environmentally sustainable cities in the country. But the more recently developing part of it—the outer boroughs and the suburbs—are on an entirely different historical arc.

WILLIAMS: On Staten Island, the West Shore is the largest swath of undeveloped real estate left on the island. There's a study that's been going on for over a year now on planning for development, but the major problem is the lack of public participation. They are doing the planning section by section and going door to door to try to get people to come to the planning meetings to discuss their ideas for how they want to see the area developed: transportation, recreation, schools, housing, industrial versus residential, retail. And whether the planning should be done on a village scale.

Finishing the Work

D. POPPER: Actually, one of the questions that I have fits in with this: Whether and how the Greenbelt, as a large, preserved area, gives a clear direction for an overall change in land preservation priorities on Staten Island.

PRATT: Well, the Parks [and Recreation] Department has had an aggressive policy of taking on new parks on the South Shore, which has the least amount of park development. And there's a great need for funding for Goodhue Woods on the North Shore. Some $30 million.

VORWICK: And, even within the Greenbelt, there are a couple of properties that are not totally protected, Pouch Camp being the main one. There's work to do yet in working with all the different land-owning entities.

D. POPPER: Are there better ways of articulating the relationships between the public and private greenspace ownerships to accomplish this? Is the Conservancy satisfied with them or are you not satisfied with them?

VORWICK: Well, in terms of Pouch Camp, the Greenbelt Conservancy and the Parks [and Recreation] Department work closely with the Scouts on offering programs. But we don't have the authority to control how they manage their property ecologically. There are a lot of wetlands, and Orbach Lake is right smack in the middle. The Amundson Trailway and the Olmsted Trailway, which are the mapped rights-of-way for Willowbrook and Richmond parkways (the White and Blue trails), are only de facto parks. I don't know of any proposal right now to actually build roads there, but I'm the kind of person, and so is the Conservancy's board, that would like to check this off the worry list.

MITCHELL: It worries me that, all these years later, you still have not been able to finish demapping those highways.

PAULO: That doesn't worry me at all because I think the way Robert Moses did this, in spite of what elected officials say, the route was not really a mapped highway corridor to begin with. Robert Moses set it up as a park improvement. The only section that was actually taken through condemnation was between Ocean Terrace and Manor Road. Along these proposed routes are wetlands and kettle ponds, which are officially mapped as such. Years ago, wetlands wouldn't stop anyone from building a highway, but you can't do that kind of thing today. I'm not saying that there shouldn't be demapping. But Willowbrook, in spite of what anyone says, simply couldn't be built. The fact is, both those right-of-ways, Willowbrook and Richmond, are now under New York City Parks's jurisdiction. Early on, I met with state officials to ask if any state planning group would ever consider building these roads. And they said to me—this is twenty years ago—"the entire state budget to maintain the road system for the state is eighty million. If you think we're gonna spend any money on Staten Island, you're crazy." So, I think the rights-of-way will be demapped eventually. But, for now, there's no interest on the part of elected officials to do any of that kind of road building.

D. POPPER: Well, it was a remarkable achievement to have saved it before the road builders got to it and to have made it into a Greenbelt. It's here, and it's wonderful. One thing that was different at the time was how many non-Staten Islanders were also engaged in defending the area—all of those walks you took, with the mayor and others coming out and walking along. How come all of these people did that?

NACHISON: People asked them to participate on a one-to-one basis. They responded to a personal request from people that they knew.

STERN: The Parks Commissioner, Thomas Hoving, was out there in 1966. Walking.

PRATT: The Protectors of Pine Oak Woods, now a 2,500-member organization, is still very focused on the Greenbelt, and we still run large numbers of walks, some in the Greenbelt, some other places. Sometimes we get as many as 100 people.

DOMINOWSKI: My particular concern is not so much that they are going to build highways. But a lot of pieces of land within what we consider to be the Greenbelt are owned by different agencies, and I'm just afraid that they may be susceptible to uses that are not compatible with the Greenbelt idea. We've seen that on Todt Hill, where all of a sudden this site became a communications tower, and you can't go near it. And it's right smack at the top of the Greenbelt.

It would be good if we could do whatever horse trading is needed to get those parcels of land ruled off limits. The High Rock story shows that titans can be defeated. You had a situation where Staten Island was undergoing tremendous change. An old way of life was suddenly disappearing. And New York had grown tired of Mr. Moses. And so, with great good luck, wonderfully energetic people prevailed.

Some Final Words

STERN: I want to say a couple of things for the record. One is I appreciate being invited here today. What you need, obviously, is wider support for an environmental agenda on the island. There are defensive battles that have to be fought as well as offensive battles to get more land. So I'm glad you had this meeting. It's like a constitutional convention. [Laughter.] Moving ahead does require working together, maybe by a membership organization or by a committee of twenty, fifty, or 100, because you need another voice on the island in addition to the traditional environmental groups. These groups are perfectly good, but, to some extent, their views can be discounted. But this group here, this meeting, is just great.

D. POPPER: Well, it is a good group, and I will certainly send an e-mail around and find out if we'd like to do that. But, for now, let me ask our editor if he has any final questions to ask.

CHARLES LITTLE: Well, we have Adena Long here, until just recently the Greenbelt's administrator, and she's been very careful not to say anything much. I'd like to ask her what she thinks remains to be done.

LONG: Actually, everyone has touched on it in one way or another. We need to ensure that the properties that are part of the Greenbelt but are not under park ownership are at least protected from development and fully joined with the Conservancy in a more formal way, such as an MOU—memorandum of understanding. I think that that's imperative, as is the continued financial support of maintenance, improvement, education, especially at High Rock, which is where it all began with the 1940s Girl Scout cottages there. So, it's important that the traditional character remains.

Another key is stewardship. The Conservancy, especially with Fresh Kills coming on line, has to foster a broadly based official stewardship because there's a very obvious elected-official disconnect right now.

STERN: It's not disconnect—it's resistance.

LONG: Well, I think that many of our politicians love the park for loving the park. But, when tough issues come into play, oftentimes they're not ready to support the Greenbelt wholeheartedly.

FLANAGAN: Absolutely.

LITTLE: Before we go, there's one other person that I would like to hear from. A success, like the Greenbelt, has many fathers, as they say. But there really is one, and he is here today: Brad Greene. Brad's leadership has been responsible for much of what has been achieved with the Greenbelt. So let me ask, Brad, do you have some parting thoughts about how it all came about?

BRAD GREENE: Well, after we had named the Greenbelt, we decided, as others have mentioned here, that we ought to have hikes. So every winter around January or February we walked across the part of the Blue Trail, which we called the Olmstead Trailway and which was actually the route of the proposed Richmond Parkway. The first hike was [in] January 1966. The next one, in '67, also in January, and the next one [in] February, and then the last one was a different route and was in March. That was the way we had of getting people acquainted with different parts of the Greenbelt and the importance of preserving it.

DOMINOWSKI: Brad, why in the world did you have to do it in the winter? [Laughter.]

GREENE: Because you could see further into the woods, you could see how important it was to preserve the trailway. And another reason was you had to struggle a little bit. It was fun, but to work together you have to struggle together. That's why we were out there in the cold. That's how it was.

D. POPPER: And that's the last word. Thank you all for coming.

A GREENBELT DIRECTORY
by Michael C. Twomey

Today, there are at least 10,000 acres of parkland managed by various city, state, federal, and non-governmental agencies on Staten Island, one of the five boroughs of New York City. An additional 2,200 acres are projected for the site of Fresh Kills Park, currently in the early stages of a development that is anticipated to reach completion no earlier than 2040.

At the center of this extensive park system lies the Staten Island Greenbelt, a conglomeration of separate green spaces that have been pieced together since 1976 to offer an almost unbroken wall of nature. Consisting of 2,800 acres (with the adjacent Fresh Kills, the total will be 5,000 acres), the Greenbelt is the direct descendant of High Rock Park and a testament to John G. Mitchell, Gretta Moulton, Brad Greene, and the many others who had the vision and tenacity to fight for the preservation of this "fine patch of wild." The Greenbelt has evolved to become New York City's largest park, and it compares favorably with any park in the nation.

Hundreds of thousands of people have enjoyed the fruits of this success, whether through a leisurely walk or more vigorous hike or by utilizing the excellent recreational facilities and educational programs that complement nature's bounty. Yet many of these resources remain unknown, even to Staten Islanders. The goal of this section of the book is to help rectify that situation by providing a brief directory that explores the present phase of this many-faceted jewel. Enjoy the Staten Island Greenbelt!

HOW TO USE THIS DIRECTORY

All entries are CAPITALIZED and listed in alphabetical order, regardless of their status within the Greenbelt system. Locations and contact information (if available) are provided at the beginning of each entry. It should be noted that not all entries are located within the official bounds of the Greenbelt, and several are private institutions; but all entries benefit from a symbiotic relationship with the Greenbelt. *Italics* indicate a cross-listing of that entry elsewhere in the directory. Page references to Marbury Brown's drawings (*Part One*) and Dorothy Reilly's photographs (front matter and *Part Two*) appear in parentheses. Contact or visit the *Greenbelt Nature Center* (see page 162) to obtain information and pamphlets concerning Greenbelt activities and a map to the *Greenbelt Trail System*.

BUCKS HOLLOW

See *Red Trail, Greenbelt Trail System.*

THE CAROUSEL FOR ALL CHILDREN

Location: Willowbrook Park. Telephone: (718) 477-0605.
Website: www.sigreenbelt.org.

Located in *Willowbrook Park* (pages 96–97) along the Eton Place entry road, this replica of a Victorian carousel was opened to the public in 1999 and is operated by the *Greenbelt Conservancy.* The carousel consists of fifty-one hand-carved mounts depicting mythical beasts, endangered species, and the more traditional carousel steed. The superstructure has been hand-painted with forty murals representing significant Staten Island landmarks. The Carousel for All Children is open to the public, and it can be reserved for private functions.

COLLEGE OF STATEN ISLAND,
CITY UNIVERSITY OF NEW YORK

Location: 2800 Victory Boulevard, Staten Island, NY 10314.
Telephone: (718) 982-2000. *Website:* www.csi.cuny.edu.

Originally built as the Willowbrook State School, the facility initially served as a military hospital during World War II and only accepted its first developmentally disabled patients in 1947. The school was closed in 1987, after a damning investigative report that aired on television, resulting in a government inquiry. In 1989, New York City purchased 204 acres of the original site, and the *College of Staten Island* (CSI) transferred its Sunnyside campus there in 1993. CSI is a member of the City University of New York (CUNY) system and the only public college on Staten Island. It has the largest campus in New York City, with large, open-space areas adjacent to the public parklands of the Greenbelt. In 2010, CSI had a student body of approximately 14,000; forty-one baccalaureate and thirteen masters degree programs taught by more than 1,200 faculty members; and doctoral programs in conjunction with the CUNY Graduate Center. The on-campus Sports and Recreation Center offers a wide range of modern sports facilities, with membership packages available to the wider Staten Island community.

DEER PARK
Location: Adjacent to Staten Island Boulevard, Staten Island, NY.

Providing a peaceful backdrop to the Michael J. Petrides High School, Deer Park offers plentiful evidence of a more violent time at the end of the last ice age some 10,000 to 12,000 years ago. Retreating glaciers tore deep ravines into the earth and randomly deposited large boulders that remain in place today. The park came under the authority of the New York City Department of Parks and Recreation in 1973 as a result of a land swap for property next to the Staten Island Expressway. In 1996, this thirty-five-acre park was formally named after a member of the John Deere agricultural equipment manufacturing family, who had owned the land during the 1800s. Deer Park has been largely left alone to nature's devices, with the exception of establishing the circuitous Blue Extension Trail (see *Greenbelt Trail System*), which traverses the ravines and deep stream beds under the cover of a thick oak forest.

FRESH KILLS PARK
Location: Adjacent to Richmond Avenue and Arthur Kill Road, Staten Island, NY.

This proposed addition to the Greenbelt consists of 2,200 acres of wetlands, meadows, shorefront, and waterways, and it is the site of the former Fresh Kills Landfill. The landfill was established in 1948 in a then-undeveloped area of tidal creeks and coastal marshes. At its peak of use, household garbage from New York City deposited at Fresh Kills totaled 29,000 tons daily. By the time the landfill received its last consignment of refuse, on March 22, 2001, four gigantic mounds had emerged, which contained approximately 150 million tons of waste. The West Mound was temporarily re-opened after the September 11, 2001, attack on the World Trade Center in lower Manhattan, during which time material was transported there from Ground Zero. Recovery workers spent ten months sifting through the material for human remains. When this task was completed, the remaining debris was covered with clean soil to a depth of at least one foot and then screened in the regular manner to prevent erosion. As a result of this recovery operation, many people believe that this area contains human remains, regardless of how miniscule they might be, and should be treated by all with the utmost reverence and respect.

An ambitious thirty-year project (2010–2040) anticipates transforming this former urban eyesore into what has been envisioned as a premier park for New York City. It is being designed carefully to combine sensitivities to the demands of nature with opportunities for a variety of recreational activities for people young and old and at all times of the year. As with the original *High Rock Park* (pages 101–103), however, controversy has already emerged concerning suggestions that urban transport routes—i.e., roadways—should be incorporated into any future development of the site. It is impossible to peer thirty years into the future or to predict the final form that Fresh Kills Park will eventually assume, but the one clear lesson that emerges from *High Rock*, the book, is that citizens, ever vigilant on Staten Island, can and should participate closely in the park planning process.

GREENBELT HEADQUARTERS
See *High Rock Park.*

THE GREENBELT NATIVE PLANT CENTER
Location: 3808 Victory Boulevard, Staten Island, NY 10314.
Telephone: (718) 370–0932. *Website:* www.nycgovparks.org.

Initially located at the intersection of Richmond Avenue and Travis Avenue in the *William T. Davis Wildlife Refuge*, the *Greenbelt Native Plant Center* quickly outgrew the facilities available at that site. In 1992, funding was allocated by the New York City Department of Sanitation to purchase the thirteen-acre Mohlenhoff farm, to which the *Greenbelt Native Plant Center* relocated and still remains. The objectives of the *Greenbelt Native Plant Center* are best outlined in the organization's mission statement that declares: "Our mission is to provide native plants and seeds from local plant populations in support of the restoration and management of many of the city's most valuable natural areas. Together with our colleagues in Parks and our partners throughout the region—local conservation, research, education, botanic, and cultural institutions—we work towards the long-term sustainability of our natural resources through programming and research to improve the conservation value of the City's parkland." The 2008 catalogue lists eleven pages of plants that are indigenous to the New York metropolitan region that have been propagated at the facility. A seed bank that fulfills all international requirements contains more than 400 species, which can be cultivated in either the twenty-four seed plots, or the four acres of irrigated containerized nursery, or the six greenhouses. The *Greenbelt Native Plant Center* is a valuable resource available to both amateur and professional horticulturists and landscapers throughout Staten Island and the greater New York City and mid-Atlantic region.

THE GREENBELT NATURE CENTER

Location: 700 Rockland Avenue, Staten Island, NY 10314-6410.
Telephone: (718) 351-3450. *Website:* www.sigreenbelt.org.

This 5,440-square-foot educational facility (pages 98–99) opened to the public in 2004. Information and pamphlets concerning all Greenbelt activities are available at this location. The Richmond County Savings Foundation Exhibit allows for a visual and tactile learning experience, and educational lectures are regularly scheduled. Additional programs include yoga, Tai-Chi, art, and photography, as well as guided hikes and story-telling sessions. The center also caters to social events, ranging from children's birthdays to weddings and dances. Maps to the *Greenbelt Trail System* may be obtained here, and access to the trails is gained via a wooden bridge aptly named "Mitchell's Crossing."

GREENBELT RECREATION CENTER

Location: 501 Brielle Avenue, Staten Island, NY 10314.
Telephone: (718) 667-3545. *Website:* www.sigreenbelt.org.

This building was the former motor garage for the Sea View Hospital and, with a surviving crematorium and a demolished mortuary that once stood to the rear, formed a complex of buildings on the present site. One would hardly envisage such a *de trop* previous existence when one enters the modernized motor garage, for it is a hive of vibrant activity. The brightly decorated modern interior offers arts and crafts, a game room, weight and cardio rooms, a computer room equipped with ten consoles, a multi-purpose room, and an aerobics/dance room. The center offers a plethora of programs, including art, music, technology, photography, dance, sport, and health and fitness activities as well as social events such as the turkey trot dance. The center's outdoor facilities are as extensive as those indoors. These include three basketball courts, two tennis courts, a soccer/lacrosse pitch, a croquet lawn, and three chess tables. While it is a public facility, a minimum annual membership fee applies, although it has been suggested that spectral visitors from the past enjoy the facilities free of charge.

GREENBELT TRAIL SYSTEM
Location: Staten Island Greenbelt, Staten Island, NY.

The Greenbelt hiking trail system consists of four main trails—Blue, Red, White, and Yellow (described below)—and eight lesser trails—Blue Extension, Green, Lavender, Nature Center, Orange, Paw, Pink, and Red Dot—encompassing more than thirty miles. Access is strictly pedestrian, as bicycles and motorized vehicles are prohibited. Visitors can obtain maps and access to some trails at the *Greenbelt Nature Center* (pages 98–99), while access to other trails is disbursed throughout the system. Withal, the Greenbelt Trail System meanders extensively, and with map in hand the hiker need not be restricted to a prescribed itinerary, for many of the trails intersect, thereby offering a wide range of circular routes. Descriptions of the four main trails follow in alphabetical order:

The Blue Trail, at 12.3 miles, is the longest within the Greenbelt Trail System. It is classified as an easy-to-moderate hike or walk over level ground. Beginning near *Sea View Hospital*, the *Blue Trail* takes a southwesterly direction through *La Tourette Golf Course* (pages 92–93) before swinging east to *High Rock Park* (pages 100–103). Then, turning in a northwesterly direction, it continues through *Deer Park*, where it exits the Greenbelt. The *Blue Trail* does not, however, terminate at the edge of the Greenbelt but extends a further 2.5 miles into an urban setting.

The *Multi-Use Trail*, which opened in 2009, is a flat pathway that welcomes both cyclists and walkers. A portion of it skirts the fairways of the *La Tourette Golf Course*. One can jump on the perimeter trail virtually anywhere along the 2.6-mile circuit, although a convenient starting point is behind *St. Andrews Church and Cemetery* in *Historic Richmond Town*.

The *Red Trail*, at four miles, resembles a lasso on the Greenbelt map and is an easy-to-moderate hike or walk. Beginning at *Historic Richmond Town*, the trail passes through the southern edge of *La Tourette Golf Course* (pages 92–93), before dividing left or right as it completes a closed circuit of *Heyerdahl Hill* and *Bucks Hollow*. As the names of these two locations suggest, the *Red Trail* circuit covers ridges and hills as well as swamp bowls and secluded hollows, allowing for a more varied experience. While walking the *Red Trail*, and despite nature's best efforts at reclamation, one is reminded that the area was once subject to human habitation. On either side of the trail, low field stone walls are periodically visible, evidence of human effort to tame the wilderness.

The *White Trail* is also an easy/moderate hike covering 7.6 miles from *Willowbrook Park* (page 96) to Great Kills Park, part of the Gateway National Recreation Area located on Staten Island's southern coast. This route dissects the center of the Greenbelt in a north-to-southeasterly axis and provides naturalists with a wide variety of landscapes.

The *Yellow Trail*, at eight miles, traverses the Greenbelt in a west-to-northeasterly direction. A moderate-to-difficult trail, it begins in *Southwest Latourette*, intersects the *White Trail* on the edge of *High Rock Park*, and continues through a section of urbanized *Todt Hill* to its terminus at *Reed's Basket Willow Park*. The trail can be started from either direction, although the trail entry into *Reed's Basket Willow Park* from *Todt Hill* has been somewhat camouflaged by a considerable number of non-native trees and shrubs, which appear to have been planted specifically at that location. One of the highlights of this trail is *Moses Mountain* (pages 88–89).

HEYERDAHL HILL
Location: Red Trail, Greenbelt Trail System.

At 241 feet above sea level, *Heyerdahl Hill* is one of the highest points on the Atlantic seaboard, and it was the site of the Heyerdahl house and an associated vineyard. The ruins of the house can be found between the *Red Trail* and *White Trail,* and one can still climb the six steps of the ten-foot-wide entryway. The rest of the structure is a jumble of low walls and collapsed reinforced concrete slabs, but the view across *Bucks Hollow* remains a treat.

HIGH ROCK PARK
Location: 200 Nevada Avenue, Staten Island, NY 10306.
Telephone: (718) 667–2165. *Website:* www.sigreenbelt.org.

The early evolution of High Rock, including its dedication in July 1965 as a public park and the 1971 U.S. Department of the Interior designation as a Natural Environment Educational Landmark, is discussed in *Part One.* In the interval since John G. Mitchell's original edition was published in 1976, *High Rock Park* has expanded and currently consists of 90.5 acres of woods, hills, trails, and ponds, including *Walker Pond* (pages 108–109) in the southeastern corner. As the foundation-stone upon which the Greenbelt was built, *High Rock Park* retains the primary focus of the enjoyment of nature with the least interference. This goal becomes evident as soon as one passes through the park's entry gate (page 83), which was designed by landscape architect Bradford Greene in honor of the park's most prominent champion, the late Gretta Moulton. The gateway, which portrays chipmunks, squirrels, turtles, and plants native to the park, was dedicated in 1995.

Educating the public regarding the intricacies and beauty of nature has ever been a goal at *High Rock Park* and continues unabated. Information boards detail the fauna and flora to be found throughout the park, and student programs are available for all ages and are augmented by teacher-orientation programs and workshops. Both Boy Scouts and Girl Scouts can earn nature-oriented merit badges, and a summer camp is also offered as well as an environmental magazine for "young naturalists." Hands-on educational lessons explore the park's diverse ecosystems, including kettle ponds such as *Pump House Pond* (page 106).

Guided hikes of varying lengths and difficulty are also available, with six hiking trails that lead to ponds, wetlands, meadows, and old-growth woods. A slightly more adventurous hike just outside the park's boundaries is one of the most visually rewarding: to the summit of *Moses Mountain* (pages 88–89), which offers unrestricted views of Staten Island and beyond.

High Rock Park is also home to the *Greenbelt Headquarters*, located in the *Tonking House*, that was built in 1921. The house has been adapted for use as the administrative offices of the New York City Department of Parks and Recreation's Greenbelt Coordinator, park naturalists and educational staff, and the staff of the *Greenbelt Conservancy*. The conservancy is a nonprofit citizens' organization founded in 1989 to work in tandem with the Department of Parks and Recreation for the administration and maintenance of the Greenbelt.

HISTORIC RICHMOND TOWN

Location: 441 Clarke Avenue, Staten Island, NY 10306.
Telephone: (718) 351-1611. *Website:* www.historicrichmondtown.org.

Once the administrative center of Staten Island, *Richmond Town* decreased in importance when the island became incorporated as one of New York City's five boroughs in 1898. After that event, many of the administrative functions previously performed at *Richmond Town* were either taken over by New York City or moved to a new municipal building constructed at St. George. In 1919, the old 1837 Greek Revival courthouse ceased to operate in a legal capacity, and this once-vigorous neighborhood fell into decline. *Historic Richmond Town* was established in 1958 as a joint venture between New York City, which owns the 100-acre site, and the *Staten Island Historical Society*, which operates the town as a living museum.

The twenty-five-acre village area contains twenty-seven buildings, some of which have been restored and are open to the public. The structures preserved within the historic village include examples of buildings covering a 300-year period; of particular interest are the Greek Revival courthouse, a seventeenth-century schoolhouse, and a nineteenth-century general store. Re-enactors demonstrate many historic trades and cooking techniques, while utilizing period tools and clothing. An onsite museum includes several exhibitions on folk art, costumes, textiles, and tools, as well as a gift shop with items and books of local interest. One easily overlooked structure in the village is the only remaining example of an early stone-arched bridge on Staten Island that spans Richmond Creek and connects Arthur Kill Road and Richmond Hill Road.

IRVING BERLIN LODGE
See *William H. Pouch Scout Camp.*

JACQUES MARCHAIS MUSEUM OF TIBETAN ART
Location: 338 Lighthouse Hill Avenue, Staten Island NY 10306.
Telephone: (718) 987-3500. *Website:* www.tibetanmuseum.org.

Founded during 1945 in two stone buildings specifically constructed to resemble a Tibetan monastery, this museum houses an extensive collection of Himalayan artifacts. Located on a relatively secluded section of *Lighthouse Hill*, the structure is less a museum than a center for meditation and reflection, and thereby it benefits from its proximity to the periphery of the Greenbelt. The museum was established by Jacques Marchais, a wealthy antique dealer with a penchant for Tibetan art and culture, despite the fact that she never actually visited the region. The exterior includes a terraced garden and pond containing fish and lotus plants. The complex won the praise of the Dalai Lama when he visited the museum in 1991.

LAKE OHRBACH
See *William H. Pouch Scout Camp.*

LA TOURETTE GOLF COURSE
Location: 1001 Richmond Hill Road, Staten Island, NY 10306.
Telephone: (718) 351-1889. *Website:* www.nycteetimes.com.

This eighteen-hole public golf course was opened in 1928 on land purchased by New York City from the La Tourette family, which had operated a farm at the location for generations. The course was redesigned in 1936 and in 1955 came under the jurisdiction of the New York City Department of Parks and Recreation. In 1973, the course was designated a New York City Landmark. The protected area includes the restored 1870 La Tourette family mansion (pages 92–93), a three-story brick structure built in the Federal style that currently serves as the course's clubhouse. In 1982, this building was included in the U.S. Register of Historic Places. *La Tourette Golf Course* is managed by the American Golf Corporation and caters to all golfing needs. The facilities are available for social events.

LIGHTHOUSE HILL

Location: A neighborhood adjacent to High Rock Park (to the north) and Rockland Avenue (to the east), Staten Island, NY.

Formerly known as *Richmond Hill*, this area of Staten Island possesses three cultural or architectural treasures nestled on its slopes, one being the *Jacques Marchais Museum of Tibetan Art*. Although a residential area, *Lighthouse Hill* benefits from being on the periphery of the Greenbelt and retains an arborous atmosphere that is absent in more heavily developed communities. The construction of the *Staten Island Range Lighthouse* (also known as the Ambrose Channel Range Lighthouse) that commenced navigational operations in 1912 is the obvious reason for the locality's change of name. This ninety-foot tall traditional lighthouse appears rather at odds with the surrounding homes, but it still operates as an automated navigational guide. Located on Edinboro Road, the lighthouse stands on a site that can be reached via the gateway to the former keeper's dwelling, now a private house. The lighthouse is an octagonal structure with a limestone base giving way to light-colored bricks, surmounted by an iron gantry at the top allowing 360-degree access. Carved above the locked and gated door is the inscription "1909 USLHE" (United States Lighthouse Establishment), indicating that the lighthouse apparently took three years to build.

On a slightly lower topographical elevation at 190 Meisner Avenue, one can find the Wyeth House, a brick Italianate Villa style house surmounted by an octagonal cupola. It is hardly surprising that this building should be constructed in such proximity to the lighthouse, because the same height advantage that allowed the lighthouse beam to be seen from afar permitted the residents of the Wyeth House spectacular views through their floor-to-ceiling windows. Built in 1856, the Wyeth house is one of the few surviving buildings in a style that was popular among wealthy, mid-nineteenth-century Staten Island denizens. The house is named after its original owner, Nathaniel J. Wyeth, a wealthy transplant from Baltimore who was a successful lawyer and represented Staten Island in the State Assembly. The house was subsequently owned by an opera singer and his partner, a landscape painter, but, when they died, the house was left vacant for several years and began to fall into disrepair. The house was reoccupied in 1978, and the new owner began a series of much-needed repairs. In 2007, the Wyeth House was designated a protected landmark by the New York City Landmarks Preservation Commission.

MORAVIAN CEMETERY

Location: 2205 Richmond Road, Staten Island, NY 10306.
Telephone: (718) 351-0136. *Website:* www.moraviancemetery.com.

In 1740, the New Dorp Moravian Church purchased an existing cemetery at this location on what is now the eastern flank of *High Rock Park* (pages 101–103). Between the years 1863 and 1895, additional land was purchased, and the original cemetery and grounds were redeveloped. The first church was built on this site during 1763 but was deconsecrated when the present church was constructed in 1845. It is currently used as an office building. Moravian Cemetery is a non-sectarian operation, privately owned by the Moravian Church of Staten Island. Situated on 113 acres of landscaped grounds with two lakes and more than eighty miles of roads and paths, Moravian provides the usual services one would expect from a cemetery regarding interment and the bereavement process. Guided public tours of the grounds are available on Sundays, but they require advance reservations, and a small entrance fee goes towards research and information expenses. The four different tours feature biographical, historical, architectural, and natural information, while also pointing out the last resting places of prominent individuals of interest. Staff members are also available to assist the public with genealogical enquiries by utilizing records dating as far back as 1867.

MOSES MOUNTAIN
Location: Yellow Trail, Greenbelt Trail System.

A 260-foot summit offering a 360-degree view (pages 88–89), this human-made pile of fill, rock, and earth was created when Robert Moses attempted to construct the Richmond Parkway over *Todt Hill*. Moses, a notorious New York City urban planner who served as Parks Commissioner, became a national figure who did much to advance road-building and bridge-building in the New York City metropolitan area. Many of New York City's inter-borough highways were built under his tenure, but his policy of pushing forward projects regardless of environmental or societal impact fell out of favor. Staten Island appears to be covered almost entirely by a forested canopy when viewed from the peak of Moses Mountain, reason enough to make the short hike.

NEW DORP (or MORAVIAN) LIGHTHOUSE
Location: 25 Boyle Street, Staten Island, NY 10306.
Website: www.lighthousefriends.com.

The *New Dorp Lighthouse* is currently a private home located in a quiet residential area nestled between *High Rock Park* (pages 100–103) and the *Moravian Cemetery*. This structure fails to comply with the regular image of how a lighthouse should look: the building is a two-story clapboard house with a forty-foot-tall, square-shaped tower protruding through the middle of its roof. The house served as a dwelling for the lighthouse keeper, and other structures on the site included a barn and oil house. Built in the 1850s to serve as a fixed, directional range light for ships traversing New York Bay from Sandy Hook, the lighthouse was updated several times before being decommissioned in 1964. The building was sold at public auction in 1974, and the purchaser took steps to prevent the building from disintegrating.

In an interesting coincidence with *Lighthouse Hill*, another example of an Italianate Villa has survived the ravages of time and increased residential development in the vicinity. The Gustave A. Mayer House (formerly the Ryers House), located on a slightly lower elevation than the lighthouse, is at 2475 Richmond Avenue. The building is a wooden structure built in 1855–1856 that features a magnificent front porch and eye-catching square cupola. After being neglected for a considerable time, this house was designated a landmark building by the New York City Landmarks Preservation Commission in 1989, and the current owners have undertaken the considerable task of reviving it to its former glory.

NEW SPRINGVILLE PARK
See *William T. Davis Wildlife Refuge*.

PUMP HOUSE POND
See *High Rock Park*.

REED'S BASKET WILLOW SWAMP
Location: Adjacent to Ocean Terrace and Emerson Court, Staten Island, NY.

Probably the most isolated of all the Greenbelt's parks, it stands alone at the northeast corner, partially surrounded by the high walls of exclusive *Todt Hill's* mansions. An attempt appears to have been made to conceal an entry into this park by planting non-native trees and shrubs. During the early 1970s, the fifty-five-acre site was acquired by New York City and in 1978 was designated a protected freshwater wetland by New York State Department of Environmental Conservation. It came under the authority of New York City Department of Parks and Recreation in 1980. The park was named for John Reed, a farmer who owned the land during the 1800s and who harvested willow bark from the swamp with which to weave baskets. One circular portion of the *Yellow Trail* (see *Greenbelt Trail System*) can (albeit with difficulty) be found within the park. Otherwise its three ponds and several swamps have remained remarkably undisturbed.

RICHMOND COUNTY COUNTRY CLUB
Location: 135 Flagg Place, Staten Island, NY 10304.
Telephone: (718) 351-0600. *Website:* info@richmondcountycc.org.

Established in 1888 by members of the Richmond County Hunt, a fox-hunting club, Richmond County Country Club (page 94) was an early proponent of golf. A nine-hole course was installed at the present location in 1897, with a second nine holes added during the following year. The course was built on the estate of a shipping magnate whose 1840s residence, completely modernized, now serves as the clubhouse (pages 94–95). Redesigned to its current configuration in 1956, the club now has an eighteen-hole, regulation-length course of 6,636 yards. Although the property was purchased by New York State in 1989 for inclusion into the Greenbelt, it was leased back for ninety-nine years at a nominal one dollar per annum and remains a private club. Additional recreational facilities include a fitness center, a pool, and an independent tennis pavilion. Four banquet rooms are also available for private and corporate functions.

RICHMOND HILL
See *Lighthouse Hill*.

SAINT ANDREW'S CHURCH AND CEMETERY
Location: 40 Old Mill Road, Staten Island, NY 10306.
Telephone: (718) 351-0900. *Website:* www.churchofstandrew-si.com.

The first St. Andrew's congregation was founded in 1708 and chartered by Queen Anne in 1713. The present structure is the third church to stand at this location. Occupied by British forces during the American Revolutionary War, the church was used as a hospital. At least two skirmishes are claimed to have occurred in its immediate vicinity. The present church was built in 1872, replacing a structure that had burned down, as had the original. The same stones were recycled to rebuild the church on the two occasions it was destroyed by fire. The current church is described as reminiscent of Norman parish churches built in twelfth-century England.

Surrounding the church is a cemetery, where the remains of many of Staten Island's earliest inhabitants are laid to rest. Reading the inscriptions on gravestones while walking through the cemetery is literally like reading a road map for Staten Island, as many of the same names occur in both. In addition to the interment of human remains, however, "all God's creatures" can find a final resting place in a designated section of the cemetery with plots holding up to four pets. Numerous public services are provided by the church, including Girl Scouts, local theatrical groups, square dancing, Tai Chi, and Sons of Italy meetings.

SEA VIEW HOSPITAL REHABILITATION CENTER AND HOME
Location: 460 Brielle Avenue, Staten Island, NY 10314.
Telephone: (718) 317-3275.
Website: www.nyc.gov/html/hhc/seaview/home.html.

The first healthcare program associated with the Sea View site began in 1829, when New York City established a poorhouse on a portion of the property, which became known as the Farm Colony. Since this facility, now largely overgrown, was located in an area behind the present *Greenbelt Recreation Center*, it appears as if the land on which Sea View Hospital was built was at one time under its jurisdiction. Together with the current site, the property totals 180 acres, with the Sea View section now under the authority of the Health and Hospitals Corporation.

In 1913, a tuberculosis hospital opened on the Sea View site. Now abandoned, the ruins of the tuberculosis health complex can be found behind a modern rehabilitation center. The complex consisted of eight buildings to house patients, an administration building, a kitchen, and a dining hall. All the patients' buildings were interconnected by covered pathways, as patients were encouraged to spend as much time as possible outside in fresh air as part of their treatment. Designed to care for a maximum of 1,682 patients, the complex held 2,000 during 1940–1941. Research was also conducted at the facility, with staff playing a significant role in developing new drugs to aid in recovery.

On June 3, 1973, a new 304-bed facility opened on the site, which provides therapy and rehabilitation, care for Alzheimer's patients, and various community-based healthcare programs. A traumatic brain-injury center was opened in 1992, and the headquarters for Staten Island's Emergency Medical Services is located on the property. A museum recently opened in the former nurses' residence, which offers pre-scheduled guided tours and contains exhibits of everyday life and medical instruments from the era of the tuberculosis complex. The *Staten Island Ballet* (www.siballet.org) is located in one of the neoclassical buildings original to this site. This 100-year-old building, which was renovated to provide modern dance facilities while retaining the building's obvious charm, received an award in 2003 from the Preservation League.

SOUTHWEST LA TOURETTE

Location: Adjacent to Richmond Avenue and Forest Hill Road, Staten Island, NY.

This portion of the Greenbelt, in concert with *La Tourette Golf Course* (pages 92–93), forms the 511-acre *La Tourette Park*. Whereas the golf course is an intensively managed greenspace, most of southern Latourette remains an unspoiled drainage basin, with Richmond Creek its dominant natural feature. As such it provides an ecologically friendly habitat for a variety of marsh and swamp life. Only on its periphery have people been allowed to intrude, and even there access is restricted. A dirt roadway that intersects with Forest Hill Road allows access to a single baseball field, which, considering its location, is appropriately named the "Field of Dreams." Continuing further along the same dirt road, one encounters a little-known gem among the Greenbelt's many recreational facilities: a grassy model airplane "airstrip." Equipped with starting tables, a covered observation shelter, and several benches, the site has provided a base of operations for the *Staten Island Radio Controlled Modelers* (www.statenislandremodelers. org) for more than thirty years. Current president Tom Abate states that more than 100 active members utilize the facility. An obliterated cemetery is thought to exist adjacent to the model airstrip, and on one occasion a club member discovered a grave marker as he sought to retrieve a model airplane that had crashed into the dense vegetation nearby. Unfortunately, subsequent attempts to locate this stone were unsuccessful, even when a global positioning device was utilized.

STATEN ISLAND BALLET

See *Sea View Hospital Rehabilitation Center and Home.*

STATEN ISLAND HISTORICAL SOCIETY

See *Historic Richmond Town.*

STATEN ISLAND RANGE LIGHTHOUSE
See *Lighthouse Hill.*

STATEN ISLAND RADIO CONTROLLED MODELERS
See *Southwest La Tourette.*

TODT HILL (pronounced Toad Hill)
Location: An exclusive residential neighborhood northeast of *High Rock Park* and *Richmond Country Club* in Staten Island known for its mansions and high elevation. See *Yellow Trail, Greenbelt Trail System; Moses Mountain;* and *Reed's Basket Willow Swamp.*

TONKING HOUSE (Greenbelt Headquarters)
See *High Rock Park.*

"UNTIL WE MEET AGAIN" MEMORIAL GARDEN
See *William H. Pouch Scout Camp.*

WALKER POND
See *High Rock Park.*

WILLIAM H. POUCH SCOUT CAMP
Location: 1465 Manor Rd., Staten Island, NY 10314.
Telephone: (718) 351-1905. *Website:* www.pouchcamp.org.

Established as the only Boy Scouts of America camp in New York City, Pouch, as it is known locally, consists of 143 acres of lakes, ponds, and woodlands and is open for Boy Scout activities year-round (page 65). During the early 1940s, Ohrbach's Department Store provided funding to construct a dam, which resulted in the present seventeen-acre Lake Ohrbach. While attempting to cause the least possible disturbance to nature, Pouch Camp offer many amenities, including camping, hiking, mountain biking, fishing, boating, archery, wall climbing, and amateur ham radio sessions. An open sports field provides opportunities to play basketball, soccer, volleyball, waffle ball, Frisbee, and other games. Camping arrangements consist of two

Camp Master cabins, seven Boy Scout cabins, approximately fifty-five lean-tos, and twenty tent sites.

Pouch Camp caters to a wide variety of Boy Scout needs, including merit badge requirements, leadership training, scouting paraphernalia, ceremonial sites, and access to the *Irving Berlin Lodge*. This structure was named for the composer Irving Berlin, who donated his proceeds from "God Bless America" to the New York City Boy Scouts. The building is available for meetings and functions and houses a computer center and a small museum containing Boy Scout memorabilia in its basement. Located directly outside the *Irving Berlin Lodge* is the *"Until We Meet Again" Memorial Garden*, a dedicated area where people can reflect on deceased friends and family members. Monuments honoring the many American war veterans, and their canine helpers, have also been erected in the memorial garden. A nondenominational open air chapel is also available within the camp grounds. The *William H. Pouch Boy Scout Camp* is utilized by troops from throughout the tri-state New York metropolitan area, as well as by troops from further afield who often use the camp's facilities as a base of operations from which they make excursions into other parts of New York City.

WILLIAM T. DAVIS WILDLIFE REFUGE

Location: 2252 Richmond Avenue, Staten Island, NY 10314.
Telephone: (718) 667-5169. *Website:* www.sigreenbelt.org.

The refuge first came into being in 1928 as a fifty-two-acre natural area and bird sanctuary called *New Springville Park*, the first of its kind in New York City. The park was expanded in 1929 when New York City bought 157.62 adjacent acres from the Crystal Water Company, which had sold bottled spring water from the site. In 1955, a nature education center was founded, marking the beginning of the sanctuary's continuous role as an educational center. It was in 1982 that *New Springville Park*, then totaling 375 acres, was renamed the *William T. Davis Wildlife Refuge* after the respected Staten Island naturalist and etymologist (page 13), who was a founding member of the Natural Association of Staten Island. Since then, the refuge has continued to expand to 814 acres. In 1987, the comparatively easy and circuitous Pink Trail of the *Greenbelt Trail System* was completed, to allow public access to the wetlands along Travis Avenue.

WILLOWBROOK LAKE

See *Willowbrook Park*.

WILLOWBROOK PARK

Location: Adjacent to Eaton Place and Richmond Avenue (to the west) and the *College of Staten Island* (to the east), Staten Island, NY.

This section of the Greenbelt extends from the main body as a narrow sliver of land flanking the *College of Staten Island*. The origins of *Willowbrook Park* (page 96) can be traced to 1909, when New York City acquired 105 acres from Staten Island Water Supply, which was subsequently assigned to the New York City Department of Parks and Recreation in 1929. A few years later, in 1932, the five-acre, human-made pond named *Willowbrook Lake* (page 107) was opened and stocked with fish. Today, catch and release fishing is allowed at *Willowbrook Lake* upon receipt of the appropriate permit, although there is a ban on all lead weights, as the lake is also designated as a bird sanctuary. During 1939 and 1940, two more tracts of land were added to the park from land formerly allocated to the abandoned Willowbrook Parkway extension. Several subsequent acquisitions of small parcels of land brought the present extent of the park to approximately 164 acres.

The periphery of *Willowbrook Park* is extensively served by recreational facilities. Five baseball fields provided with ample parking are located at the northeastern border of the park within sight of the *College of Staten Island*, and six tennis courts can be found on the eastern side of *Willowbrook Lake* near the Eton Place entrance. This area also contains the *Carousel for All Children* (page 97) and, perhaps, the only public outdoor archery range on Staten Island. Despite serving as an unofficial dog run during the early morning, the archery range enjoys extensive usage in the evening hours.

A terminus of the Greenbelt's *White Trail* (see *Greenbelt Trail System*) is located at the northern end of *Willowbrook Park*, and, if one were to walk a short distance along this trail, one would encounter, standing next to a stream, a ruined structure that is possibly a relic from Willowbrook's early industrial days. During the 1760s, Willowbrook had several metal-working factories, and the ruins in question, consisting of a hearth and a sturdy chimney, possibly served such a purpose.

NOTES TO PART ONE

Tracks

1. This version, according to Leng and Davis, was disputed in 1856 by a correspondent for the semi-weekly *Staten Islander*. Todt, the anonymous writer claimed, was in fact a vernacular perversion of Toad. It seems a young man in days of yore was courting a lovely woman who lived on the hill, but the affection was not reciprocal. "In order to cause him to discontinue his unwelcome visits," Leng and Davis quote the story as claiming, "she privately dropped a toad or two . . . into his capacious pockets, where they remained until they became offensive."

2. In a doctoral thesis on the limonite mines of Staten Island, Irving Glaser reports that the British barely scratched the surface of the ore deposits. From 1830 to 1885, an estimated 300,000 tons of ore were extracted from scattered mine sites in the serpentine, including several then located on the Todt Hill slope at the edge of the Richmond County Country Club golf course, not far from High Rock.

3. Kenneth Scott, writing in the Spring 1955 *Proceedings* of the Staten Island Institute of Arts and Sciences, reports that, upon their return to the island in 1783, the Broome brothers retained Aaron Burr as their attorney and filed an action against Conner for trespass. Conner was found guilty and fined a nominal sum. Though some historians considered him a Tory, Scott notes that Conner was a member of the Committee of Safety in 1776 and no doubt was "a convinced patriot."

The Race for Space

1. In a paper published in the March 1965 edition of *The New Bulletin* (S.I. Institute of Arts and Sciences), Bradford Greene traces the origin of the Greenbelt concept to Queen Elizabeth I, who in 1580 decreed that a rural belt be created around London to harness its growth. Green also credits Maniscalco with introducing the term on Staten Island. In an interview in 1975, Maniscalco told me he first used the word in an executive session of the Board of Estimate, probably late in 1963. "It was before High Rock," he said. "I was telling them we shouldn't repeat on Staten Island all the mistakes of the other boroughs. And all of a sudden it just came out. I said, 'We have this marvelous Greenbelt.' And (Mayor Robert) Wagner looked over at me and said, 'I like that, Al. That's got a nice ring to it.'" Maniscalco acknowledged, however, that, while he did not himself invent the word, neither did he purloin it from Queen Elizabeth: "I think I heard it a few months earlier at some party. Someone was quoting some

nineteenth-century author." Could that person possibly have been Gretta Moulton? I asked. "I don't recall," Maniscalco replied. "But, now that you mention it, it could have been."

2. In his heyday of power, Robert Moses was a wearer of many hats. Simultaneously in the late 1950s and early 1960s, he had served as the chairman of the Triborough Bridge and Tunnel Authority, of the State Council of Parks, of the State Power Authority, and as New York City Construction Coordinator, among a number of other appointive posts. More than any mayor ever elected—more than any *individual*, Moses shaped the New York City that we know today. In the words of his critical biographer, Robert Caro, with his power Moses "influenced the destiny of all the cities of twentieth-century America."

Getting from Here to There

1. So many different numbers (not to mention different consultants) have come up over the years, designating so many different alternates, that it would be reckless and stultifying to account for them all here. For clarity, we shall refer only to three: the Original Route (the Moses alignment), Alternate Four (the Ballard-Palmer route, or variations thereof), and Alternate Six (a variation of the Original Route).

More Perils, More Friends

1. In 1971, on behalf of the institute, the Parks and Recreation Department retained the firm of Clarke and Rapuano to prepare a master plan for the institute's anticipated expansion. The plan centered on the possible consolidation of institute activities in a complex of buildings at Ft. Wadsworth (contingent on the U.S. Defense Department declaring the property surplus). There was a second contingency in the plan: construction of a 30,000-square-foot "environment center" to house all of the institute's science activities, with parking space for 105 visitor-vehicles and forty staff. The center was to be located at High Rock, near Walker Pond. Some of the institute's directors objected. While recognizing the institution's legitimate hope for additional space somewhere, not to mention High Rock's need for a small visitor-orientation building at Walker Pond, the critics wondered why a nature conservation center should be selected as the possible site for so large a facility. Some also wondered why parking for 145 additional cars should detract from the park's unspoiled acreage when a lot for some seventy-five cars and six buses had just been completed nearby, off Summit Avenue. (That lot, incidentally, was designed with great sensitivity for Clarke and Rapuano by Bradford Greene. Among other things, Green's design obliterated all ugly traces of New Dorp Garden's premature foundations and at the same time avoided encroaching on a superb grove of mixed conifers planted decades earlier by Warren Walker.) In any event, Sailors Snug Harbor soon became the focus of the institute's consolidation plans, and the "environmental center" for High Rock was promptly dispatched to the trash can.

BIOGRAPHICAL NOTES
Part One (1976)

JOHN G. MITCHELL, the author of *High Rock: A Natural and Unnatural History*, herein republished as *Part One*, lived on Staten Island from 1958 to 1977. He was the founder of SIGNAL (Staten Island Greenbelt-Natural Areas League) and a major figure not only in saving High Rock Camp from development, but also in creating the Staten Island Greenbelt. After graduating from Yale University in 1954, he was a newspaper reporter in Massachusetts, New Mexico, and California, finally winding up at the *Journal American* in New York City. Soon after, he became the science editor for *Newsweek* magazine, where he was the first to cover environmental issues on a regular basis. He was the founding editor of *Open Space Action* magazine and in 1970 became the editor-in-chief for Sierra Club Books. He moved to Connecticut in the mid-1970s, where he was a Mellon Fellow at Yale University's School of Forestry, a sought-after freelancer, and a field editor for *Audubon* magazine. In 1994, he went to Washington, D.C., as the environment editor for *National Geographic* magazine, where his vivid journalism reached tens of millions of readers. He returned to Connecticut in 2004 but continued writing and editing for *National Geographic*, *Smithsonian*, and other educational publications. He is the author of hundreds of magazine articles and eight acclaimed books, among them *Losing Ground* (Sierra Club Books, 1975), *The Hunt* (Alfred A. Knopf, 1980), *Alaska Stories* (Academy Chicago Publishers, 1984), *The Man Who Would Dam the Amazon and Other Accounts from Afield* (University of Nebraska Press, 1990), and *Dispatches from the Deep Woods* (University of Nebraska Press, 1992). John Mitchell died of a heart attack in July 2007 while returning home to Old Lyme, Connecticut, from a family place in the Adirondacks.

MARBURY BROWN, the illustrator for *High Rock*, lived on Staten Island from 1960 through 1973, after which he and his wife, Dorothy, retired to their summer place in Nederland, Colorado. He died in Colorado in 1997. After studying at the Jepson Art School in Glendale, California, and later at the Kansas City Art Institute, Marbury Brown became well known for his sophisticated men's fashion illustrations for Bergdorf Goodman, Nieman Marcus, Saks Fifth Avenue, and others. Regarded as one of the most successful fashion illustrators of the 1960s and 70s, he was a Dolphin Fellow of the American Watercolor Society, winning the Society's top award in 1968, and taught at Washington University in St. Louis, the University of North Carolina at Chapel Hill, and the Pratt Institute in Brooklyn. His paintings, drawings, and watercolors are in the permanent collections of fine art museums throughout the United States and in private collections.

ROBERT HAGENHOFER designed and produced the original edition of *High Rock*. He was a co-founder and president of the Staten Island Citizens Planning Committee, which was the first to advance the idea of a greenbelt, and he was active in the preservation of open space elsewhere on the island. After graduating from the Chicago Institute of Design, he served with the U.S. Army in Europe during World War II, then opened a freelance design practice in Manhattan. He later worked in the Graphics Department at the College of Staten Island and at Middlesex Country College in Edison, New Jersey. In New Jersey, he was a founder of the Sourland Regional Citizens Planning Council and worked on protecting Sourland Mountain, located between Princeton and Flemington, from inappropriate development. A book he designed and produced, *The Sourland Legacy* (1989), with illustrations by Marbury Brown and text by John G. Mitchell and Charles E. Little, won special recognition from Somerset County for helping to preserve this historic area. Robert Hagenhofer lived on Staten Island from 1952 until 1977, when he moved to New Jersey. He died at his home in Hillsborough in November 2007.

Part Two (2011)

ALISON C. MITCHELL, who conceived of this republication project, attended Vassar College and the College of Staten Island and earned a master's degree in human resources development at Antioch University. She is the recipient of a Woman of Achievement Award from the *Staten Island Advance* (1968), the *Connecticut Magazine* Award for Distinguished Service (1981), and a Distinguished Faculty Award from the University of Bridgeport (1993). In New York, she was a member and vice chair of the New York City Arts Commission. After moving to Connecticut in 1978, she was the executive director of the YWCA in Bridgeport, Connecticut. In 1994, she relocated to Washington, D.C., where her husband, John, was the environment editor at *National Geographic* magazine. She taught at the Northern Virginia Community College and served as an archivist at the Air and Space Museum of the Smithsonian Institution and the Folk Life Center of the Library of Congress. She now makes her home in Old Lyme, Connecticut.

CHARLES E. LITTLE, project editor, is the author of fifteen acclaimed books on land conservation and the environment, among them *Greenways for America* (The Johns Hopkins University Press, in association with the Center for American Places, 1990), *Discover America: The Smithsonian Book of the National Parks* (Smithsonian Books, 1995), *The Dying of the Trees: The Pandemic in America's Forests* (Viking, 1995), *Sacred Lands of Indian America* (Harry N. Abrams, 2001), and *The Encyclopedia of Environmental Studies, Second Edition* (Facts on File, 2001). He is also the president of the American Land Publishing Project, founding editor of *Voices from the American Land*, a new poetry chapbook series, and an adjunct faculty member in the Department of Geography at the University of New Mexico. While living in New York City, he was the executive director of the Open Space Action Committee (now Open Space Institute) and worked with the original "Ad hoc Committee on Camp High Rock Site" during the mid-1960s. He moved to Washington, D.C., in 1972, and was, in turn, a senior associate at the Conservation Foundation, the head of Natural Resources Policy Research at the Congressional Research Service of the Library of Congress, and the founder and first president of the American Land Forum, a policy research organization in Washington, D.C. In 1994, he moved with his wife, Ila Dawson Little, a professor emerita of English, to Placitas, New Mexico.

DOROTHY REILLY provided the photographic images for the front matter and *A Greenbelt Gallery* and wrote the captions. She has chronicled the Greenbelt with her camera for nearly a decade and has undertaken landscape photography in the Himalayas, British Columbia, and throughout the northeastern United States. A native Staten Islander, she graduated from Wagner College and holds a master's degree in art and education from Columbia University. She works as the director of public relations for the Greenbelt Conservancy.

MICHAEL C. TWOMEY, historian, prepared *A Greenbelt Directory*. A native of Ireland, he is currently completing the first book of a two-part series on the Irish Revolution in County Cork, 1916–1921. After emigrating to New York in 1989, he became a New York City paramedic, for which he has received numerous awards, and was on the scene after the September 11, 2001, attack on the World Trade Center. Currently an adjunct lecturer with the Department of History at the College of Staten Island, he resides on Staten Island with his wife, Deborah Loperfido Twomey, a staff member at Wagner College, and their son, Hugh.

DEBORAH E. POPPER organized and moderated *A Greenbelt Forum*, and she has been an editorial consultant on the republication project. She is a professor of political science, economics, and philosophy at the City University of New York, College of Staten Island, acting director of CSI's Honors College, and a visiting professor at Princeton University's Environmental Institute. A graduate of Bryn Mawr, she has a master's degree in library science from Rosary College and a master's degree and doctorate in geography from Rutgers University. In 1997, she won the coveted Paul P. Vouras Medal of the American Geographical Society for her work on regional geography. She lives with her husband, Frank J. Popper, a professor of urban and regional planning at Rutgers University, in Highland Park, New Jersey.

GEORGE F. THOMPSON, publisher, is the founder and director of the Center for American Places, a nonprofit publishing organization now lodged at Columbia College Chicago. A former acquisitions editor for the Johns Hopkins University Press, he founded the Center in 1990 and since then has brought more than 350 books to publication, winning more than 100 awards and prizes, including best-book honors in thirty-one academic fields. In 2000, he won the Publications Award of the Association of American Geographers, in 2002 a Publications Commendation from the Vernacular Architecture Forum, and in 2005 the Communications Award of the Council of Educators in Landscape Architecture. He is an author and editor of five books, including *Landscape in America* (University of Texas Press, 1995), which was designated a Notable Book of 1995 by *Harper's* magazine, and (with Frederick R. Steiner) *Ecological Design and Planning* (John Wiley, 1997; 2007). He lives in Staunton, Virginia, with his wife, Cynthia Thompson, a professor of dance at James Madison University, and their daughter, Haley.

ABOUT THE BOOK

High Rock and the Greenbelt: The Making of New York City's Largest Park is the twenty-second volume in the Center Books on American Places series, George F. Thompson, series founder and director. The book was brought to publication in an edition of 1,250 hardcover copies with the generous financial support of Eva Baez, Burnham Carter, Jr., Daniel M. and Mary Jane Davis, Mary L. Greene, Sheila Hagenhofer, Alison C. Mitchell, Pamela Mitchell, Louise Petosa, Fare R. Radin, Jean G. Roland, Elizabeth M. Seder, Rose M. Volpe, and the Friends of the Center for American Places, for which the publisher is most grateful.

The epigraph on page v comes from Aldo Leopold, *A Sand County Almanac and Sketches Here and There* (New York and Oxford: Oxford University Press, 1949), 176–77. The text was set in New Baskerville, the paper is 140 gsm Gold East matte art, and the book was printed and bound in China. For more information about the Center for American Places at Columbia College Chicago, please see page 198.

FOR THE CENTER FOR AMERICAN PLACES
AT COLUMBIA COLLEGE CHICAGO

George F. Thompson, *Founder and Director*
Brandy Savarese, *Editorial Director*
Jason Stauter, *Operations and Marketing Manager*
Erin F. Fearing, *Executive Assistant*
Melissa L. Jones, *Editorial Assistant*
Purna Makaram, *Manuscript Editor*
Ila Little, *Proofreader*
David Skolkin, Book *Designer and Art Director*

Center for American Places

AT COLUMBIA COLLEGE CHICAGO

The Center for American Places at Columbia College Chicago is a nonprofit organization, founded in 1990 by George F. Thompson, whose educational mission is to enhance the public's understanding of, appreciation for, and affection for the places of the Americas and the world—whether urban, suburban, rural, or wild. Underpinning this mission is the belief that books provide an indispensable foundation for comprehending and caring for the places where we live, work, and commune. Books live. Books are gifts to civilization.

Since 1990 the Center for American Places at Columbia College Chicago has brought to publication more than 350 books under its own imprint and in association with numerous publishing partners. Center books have won or shared more than 100 editorial awards and citations, including multiple best-book honors in more than thirty fields of study.

For more information, please send inquiries to the Center for American Places at Columbia College Chicago, 600 South Michigan Avenue, Chicago, Illinois 60605-1996, U.S.A., or visit the Center's Website (www.americanplaces.org).